STATUES OF REVELATION

The strange Easter Island statues stand aloof to the passing aeons, their eyes gazing at sights which today's living beings cannot see . . . sights of wonder and terror, creation and destruction which began and ended long before our day.

The statues' secrets, like the wind which blows across the island, are elusive – but Jean-Michel Schwartz has penetrated the forgotten mysteries of the Islanders' cryptic *rong-rongo* writing, to unlock the lost past of Easter Island and the vanished race which lived there amid the timeless secrets of the cosmos.

Also in this series in Sphere Books:

THE SECRETS OF STONEHENGE

The Secrets of Easter Island

JEAN-MICHEL SCHWARTZ

Translated from the French by Lowell Blair

SPHERE BOOKS LIMITED
30/32 Gray's Inn Road, London WC1X 8JL

First published in Great Britain by Sphere Books Ltd 1979

TRADE
MARK

Printed in Great Britain by
Hazell Watson & Viney Ltd
Aylesbury, Bucks

Beyond the silence of Matakiterani

CONTENTS

TABLE OF TRANSCRIPTIONS

The lines below are taken from two pages of the Tomenika manuscript. To the left of each line is the number of the chapter in which I have translated it.

CHAPTER

Ure vae inu

IX

X

VI

VI

VII

VII

XI

IV

I

II

III

V

XII

XIII

PROLOGUE

It will be a long journey. On the way, things will happen in the mind of things. Here and there, little by little, progressively, the second meaning will appear, after the first.

Noncontradictory elements inseparable from a whole. In the image and on the scale of the great statues of the island: what they looked at was as real and fundamental as what was behind their backs.

CHAPTER ONE

The Statues of Easter Island

Ever since its discovery in 1722 by the Dutchman Roggeveen, Easter Island has intrigued and fascinated those who study it. It was reported by the pirate Davis in 1686. Others tried to find "Davis's Land," without success.

Later a strange phenomenon occurred: Easter Island seemed to have disappeared, because its magnetism is so strong that it deflects compasses, and without the necessary correction there is a risk of never reaching it.

But it is really there. An old legend of the island says, "Easter Island has not changed since ancient times." Sailors and seekers were drawn to that remote "end of the earth" after Roggeveen. Among others: Katherine Routledge in 1914, Alfred Métraux in 1934, Thor Heyerdahl in 1956, and Francis Mazière, who spent a year on the island, in 1964.

Easter Island is known by its statues. Gigantic statues weighing several tons, on a little island fifteen miles long and ten miles wide, in the middle of the Pacific. Pierre Loti wrote, "There are two kinds of statues. First, those on the beaches, which have been toppled and broken. Then the others, from a different time and with different faces, which still stand on the other side of the island, in the depths of a solitude no longer penetrated by anyone."

Yes, it is primarily because of its statues that Easter Island is famous and fantastic. The massacres have been forgotten, along with the fact that in 1862 nearly all its inhabitants, including its "scholars" and its last initiates, were rounded up by Peruvian slave traders and taken off to die in guano mines off the coast of Peru. It was a strange turn of fate if we accept the idea that one of the first importations of civilization to the island came from South America, and perhaps precisely from Peru, before the Polynesian migration of King Hotu Matua, whose memory is still preserved in many legends.

But the statues have remained. They are actually of three types:

—Those erected at the foot of the volcano, the frightening ones; from the first period.

—Those that were moved to the shore; from the second period.

—Those from the earliest period, different and strange, which bear such a strong resemblance to certain statues in South America.

The more stories were told, the greater the mystery became.

With regard to the statues of the second period, how were they moved several miles from the place where they were made? What did they look at, and what was their meaning? How were their stone hats, some of which weigh four or five tons, placed on their heads?

And what is the meaning of the unique Easter Island writing carved into wooden tablets?

All these unanswered questions, raised by an island that is a melting pot containing elements from a grave, heavy past, require new hypotheses. I will present such hypotheses in this book.

THE GREAT STATUES OF THE ISLAND

A number of them lie in apparent disorder, in all stages of completion, on the slopes of the Rano Raraku volcano. Some enormous ones, more than sixty feet long, are ready to "come alive."

Others stand at the foot of the volcano. The wind has blown earth around them until, now, only their heads show above the ground. They have no eyes, but their empty sockets give the impression of a gaze that varies with the position of the sun. Thrust into the ground on tapered bases, they were destined, says Francis Mazière, to remain near the volcano, looking for Hiva, the "continent" that sank beneath the sea and was the original homeland of Hotu Matua, first king of the island. They also have part of the world under their dominion. And Mazière was told that those facing southward "keep the forces of the Antarctic winds and transmit their power to an enormous red volcanic stone which limits the triangle of the Pacific islands."

Finally there are those which were erected on stone

platforms called *ahus* and later overthrown. They are far from the volcano and near the sea, to which their backs were turned. They wore cylindrical hats of red volcanic stone as a sign of Knowledge. Their gaze was different from that of the preceding statues. Once they had been brought to their final location, eyes were carved for them, but only at the last moment. They were transported blind, and only at the last stage did they see what living beings cannot see.

Each *moai* (statue) was carved out of the volcano itself, with stone tools, until it was connected only by a thin ridge along its back. This ridge was then broken, and the statue, held by ropes wrapped around a stone winch carved from the wall of the crater, was lowered along passages that can still be seen today. At the foot of the volcano it was placed upright. Its back was then polished and signs were carved into it, including the circle of knowledge and initiation.

The transportation of those statues weighing several tons is a mystery. To reach the *ahus* waiting for them, they sometimes had to cover a distance of ten miles, before having their eyes opened. Finally they were erected at funerary places, *ahus*, where kings and initiates were buried after their bodies had been exposed nearby for a long time.

The transportation of the red stone hats is also a mystery. They were taken from another volcano, Puna Pau.

All this applies to the statues of the second period. For the moment, I will deal only with them.

TRANSPORTATION OF THE STATUES

On this point, tradition is unequivocal and unchanging. The Easter Islanders have said the same thing to all visitors in all times. Although the statues and the hats came from different places, they both moved from their volcanoes to their final locations by means of *mana*, a mystic, supernatural force possessed only by two initiated priests. The statues moved upright, turning in semicircles as they went.

Across that volcanic terrain, they followed known paths to the sea, on which they turned their backs. Their eyes looked at something other than what was seen by the statues that remained at the foot of the volcano and were not given the hat of Knowledge.

There have been endless theories attempting to explain how the statues were transported, but they all fail to take into account what is specifically stated by legend: that the statues moved upright, by means of *mana*, turning in semicircles. They also fail to reckon with the means known to have been at the Easter Islanders' disposal.

One theory involves wooden sledges on which the statues were placed horizontally. But no trees growing on the island were big and strong enough for that. The little *toro miro* trees, stunted by the wind, could not have supplied wood for sledges or rollers.

Another theory is that the statues were slid over a layer of sweet potatoes! But legend says that they moved upright and turning; they were never pulled in a horizontal position. At their final locations they show no trace of scratches or accidental marks of any kind; except for their eyes, they arrived finished and perfectly polished.

We must listen to what Francis Mazière says in his book *Mysteries of Easter Island.* An old Easter Islander told him about a bridge of ropes connecting two volcanoes. Was this simply a story for travelers? Even if it was, it contained one element which, in the old man's mind, could not be placed in doubt: ropes.

When Mazière discovered stone winches on Rano Raraku, the quarry volcano, he saw that they had deep grooves worn into them by ropes.

And he found the ancient grass of the island: long and extremely tough, capable of forming strong ropes. It now grows only on a little island at the foot of the Orongo cliff, the sacred place of the birdman cult. It has disappeared from the rest of Easter Island, whose plant life has changed and been altered by sheepherding.

The stones have remained. And the ancient Easter Islanders were masters in the art and technique of sculpture. The ropes, except for a few slight traces, have disappeared, but the ancient Easter Islanders were also masters in the handling of ropes. *They used ropes for transporting the statues.*

To move a statue upright and turning, there is no other way than to wrap ropes around it and have one group of men pull on one side of it while another group pulls back a little less strongly on the other.

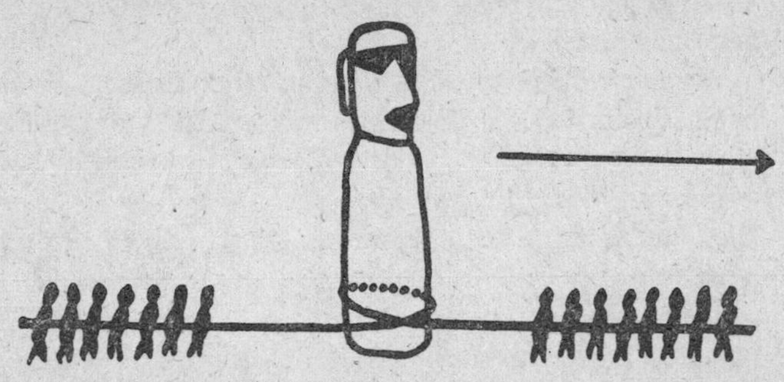

Those who pull forward make the statue move toward its destination; those who pull back (while allowing the movement to take place, which is why they must pull a little less strongly than the others) help to keep the statue in vertical balance.

The statue thus acts as a mobile winch and its weight is "diminished." It is both a pulley and the object being pulled. The force of friction is limited to its base. The statues that were moved had a round, slightly convex base, unlike those that remained near the volcano: they had a tapered base.

They turned in semicircles, first in one direction, then in the other, recalling the footsteps of a man. To achieve this, the system of ropes around the statue was double and symmetrical.

This is in accordance with legend. Since there were two initiated priests, there was a system of ropes on each side of the statue, each under the control of one of the priests.

Everyone engaged in transporting the statue believed in *mana*, for as it moved forward its weight was entirely changed by the paired forces that alternately acted on it.

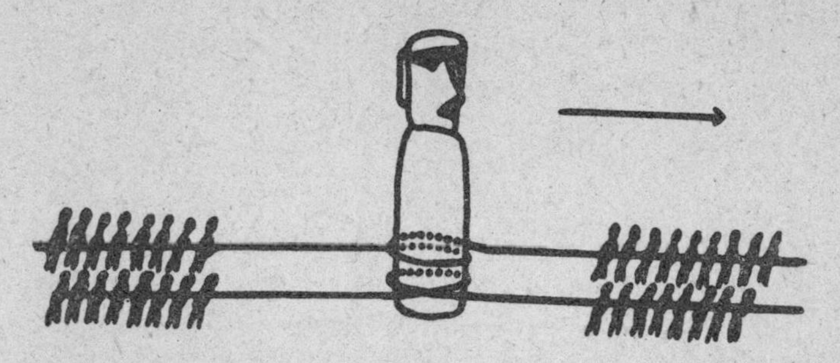

Thus, as Easter Island legend says, the statue moved upright and turning: each team alternately gave it a semicircular forward motion.

I am, of course, only indicating a general principle here; the number of men and ropes on each side varied with the weight and size of the statue.

Who were the people who created those statues in ancient times? I see Easter Island simply; clans, tribes, division and disintegration came later, but originally there were only two social classes in that closed and isolated world:

—The Long-Ears (Hanau Eepe): priests, initiates, kings, sculptors. Their name came from the fact that they stretched their earlobes by means of heavy bone weights.

—The Short-Ears (Hanau Momoko): the common people, those who worked in the quarries of Rano Raraku and Puna Pau.

The Short-Ears supplied the enormous labor of transporting the statues and putting the stone hats in place. Clans did not become important until much later, for otherwise each tribe would have undertaken its own statuary in the part of the island that it occupied, whereas the fact is that the statues were an enterprise in which everyone was involved, both in ancient times, before the arrival of Hotu Matua, and in the more recent times of the statues known as those of the second period.

In this context, *mana* was an absolute "necessity." Those who were not employed in the work of the statues and saw them moving forward from a distance (perhaps they were kept away by a taboo) could not fail to believe in *mana*, because the men and ropes seemed insignificant in relation to the sight of a stone giant slowly walking toward the sea. Those who had taken part in the work were well aware of the enormous effort that had been required, and now all at once the stone figure was moving, defying the weight and hardness which they had so vividly felt in shaping it and lifting it upright.

At this point I must make a digression. It concerns the times in the "life" of a statue when *mana* is mentioned by Easter Island tradition. It is mentioned with regard to the transportation of the statue and its hat, and nothing else. Nothing is said about it in relation to the work of carving the statue, lowering it to the foot of the volcano or lifting it upright. We have the impression that *mana*, that divine, supernatural force of the initiated priests, is not used as an explanation when understandable human work is enough to account for what is done. But when a statue acting as a pulley seems to become lighter as it slowly moves forward, the presence and power of *mana* are felt.

That is why the concept and operation of the double system of ropes, as I described it above, were linked to knowledge and initiation. Perhaps this explains why the system has till now remained unrevealed, and why the present Easter Islanders have been unable to speak of it. We will see later who gave the sculptors the idea of moving their statues in that way.

But aside from all these considerations, the work of the statues was religious, magic and enveloped in a taboo. *Mana*, the mystic, supernatural force, was therefore obligatory and absolute. It was a necessity. It was necessity itself. Without it, nothing would have had any meaning on Easter Island.

But it is a mistake to think of *mana* as a means of producing some sort of mysterious levitation. If the statues had really been moved by such levitation, would the Easter Islanders ever have dared to overthrow all of them, or at least those that had been moved, as they in fact did? That seems to me unthinkable.

THE OVERTHROWING OF THE STATUES

The statues were consecrated to worship of the dead. Moreover, the Easter Islanders attributed life and *mana* to them. Why, then, did work on the slopes of Rano Raraku stop so abruptly that the statues remained unfinished, with stone tools scattered on the ground beside them? Why were all those that had been moved to the seaside overthrown? Several thoughts come to mind.

These statues looked at the realm of the dead and of death, since they looked up at the stars and an old Easter Island legend says that the dead return to the stars in the vault of the sky. But they were consecrated only to the dead of the Long-Ears. They all have long ears.

In the development of the statues, only their size changed significantly. With a few exceptions, particularly in the case of statues from the earliest period, their shape did not vary. But their size increased drastically.

Can it be that as they became larger and larger the system of ropes was no longer capable of moving them? Or that, having become higher, so that their center of gravity was raised, not only could they no longer be moved, but they also began falling?

Mana no longer existed. Now that they had been freed from that absolute taboo, the Short-Ears saw only their enormous work, the hardships they had endured in carrying out that colossal task, and their total subjection to their masters, the Long-Ears.

They rebelled, wiped out the Long-Ears (whom they killed in the ditch on the Poike Peninsula of the island, according to legend) and overthrew the statues which were not meant for the worship of their own dead, but for which they had suffered so much. They stopped work abruptly. Then began what is known as the "statue-overthrowing time."

And so civil war ended the era of statues endowed with life and *mana*. Those stone giants, who saw the dead, died of having become too large, of having tried to see too high, too far. They had to fall; they were toppled like ordinary stones. They lost their life when they lost the *mana* that could no longer move them. They were killed by being pulled down to the ground. And later, no one remembered it.

But let us go back and accompany the giants one last time toward their goal and their destiny. The *ahu* that awaited them was made of stone slabs, with a slope leading up to the platform on which they would stand. They climbed that slope in the same way they walked, except that they were now held in balance by a rope around the neck, pulled downward on the other side of the *ahu*.

Between the slope and the platform is an angle, a step. It was made after the statue had been put in place; before, there was an unbroken rise, if only at one spot.

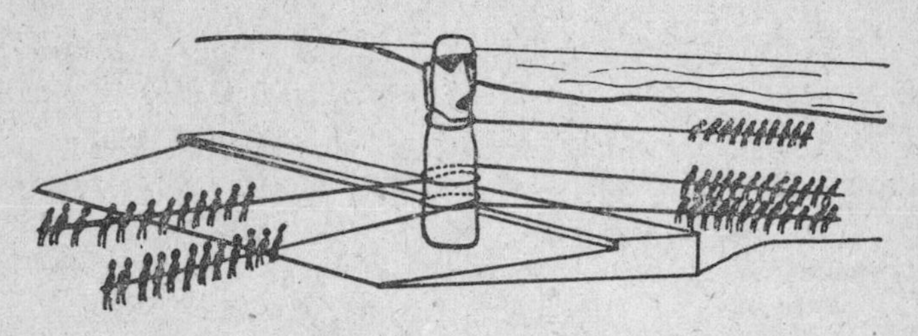

This long, sloping part of the *ahu* represents something that had already been used in many other civilizations: the ramp of stone or earth.

LIFTING THE HATS

Once it was installed on its *ahu*, the giant received the sign of Knowledge: a cylindrical hat made of red volcanic stone, sometimes weighing four or five tons, adorned with carvings. Its lower part had a recess designed to fit over the flat head of the statues.

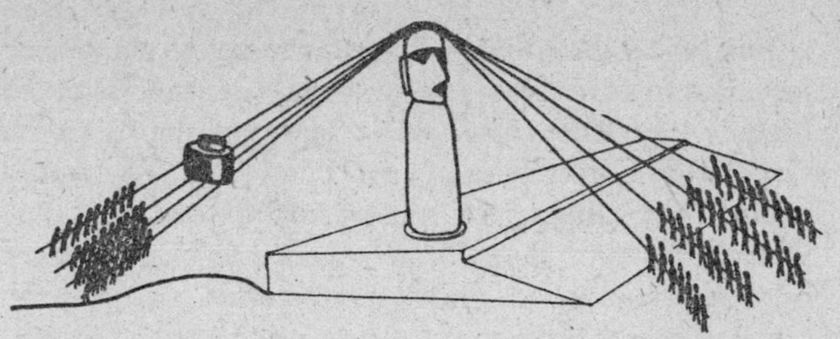

On this ramp of ropes, the hat was raised by means of a stone winch to which it was attached.

fixed rope

mobile rope

stone winch

rope attaching the hat to the winch, while enabling the winch to turn

ramp of ropes

How were those hats raised to the top of the gigantic statues? This time there were no ramps of stone or earth. As we have seen, work stopped suddenly in the quarries of Rano Raraku and Pana Pau. The sculptors' tools still lie on the ground and the statues are in various stages of completion; everything has remained in place, abandoned. But near the *ahus* there are no ramps that could have been used for raising the hats. Mazière says specifically that he found no trace of any such ramps. Furthermore we may assume that earth is scarce on that island with a volcanic subsoil. And it would have taken a ramp several dozen yards long for each statue. No.

The Easter Islanders did use a ramp, but it was composed of a bridge of ropes passing over the flat head of the statue and supported by it. The ropes were pulled taut on both sides of the statue. Those on which the hat rested were connected at a fixed distance from each other.

The ropes that worked the winch were also supported by the head of the statue, and were pulled on the other side. Movement was imparted to the winch by a mobile rope, while another rope was held fixed. As the winch turned it rose, moving the hat attached to it.

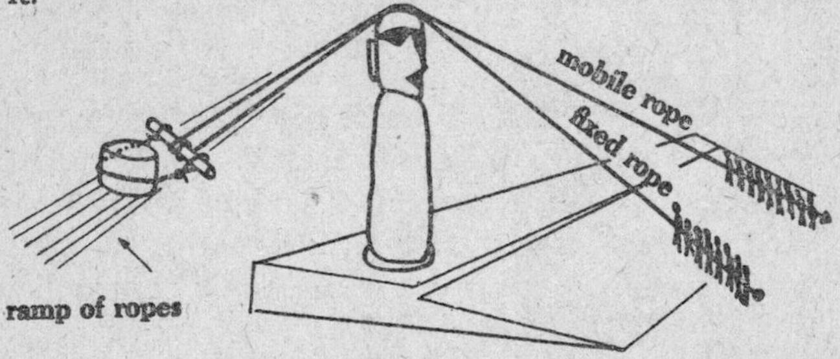

All that was erected, and it was all overthrown. It is known that the furor of overthrowing the statues was at its peak in the late eighteenth and early nineteenth centuries, the period when tribal wars were in full swing. But when did it begin, and when did work end? Those questions are harder to answer. In any case the overthrowing of the "idols" preceded in an almost prophetic way the tragedy of 1862, when the Easter Islanders were taken away to guano mines off the coast of Peru. A thousand of them died there. The fifteen survivors who were finally allowed to return to their homeland brought smallpox with them. It decimated the population that had been able to remain on the island and hastened the final decline of that civilization.

RONGO-RONGO WRITING

The writing of Easter Island, known as *rongo-rongo* writing, is found nowhere else. It has not been deciphered. Only about twenty tablets of it now exist, most of them carved on *toro miro* wood. On paper, only one manuscript is known. It is said to have been transcribed by Tomenika, one of the last initiates, and is now in Francis Mazière's possession. He has published a photograph of one of its pages in his book *Mysteries of Easter Island.*

Can the hypotheses that I have stated earlier, insofar as they are plausible, provide a key for deciphering that writing?

Let us suppose that the key is the system of transporting the statues, with the intervention of *mana.* From that viewpoint, one line of the Tomenika manuscript is particularly noteworthy. Here is a reproduction of it, including its punctuation:

The two vertical arrows indicate the place where reading will begin. The horizontal arrow shows that reading will be from right to left.

Does this segment of a line summarize what you have previously read?

As a fundamental preamble I will state the following. *Each sign representing a circle refers to initiation and knowledge. By extension it designates the hats, emblem of that knowledge. But above all it is the symbol of* mana, *the mystical force.*

He died and a *moai* (statue) was made for him.

. A master sculptor marked the outline of the statue by making holes in the stone, closely and regularly spaced. This is known and can be seen in the case of statues that have remained unfinished, as Mazière reports.

The lines of the symbol suggest a network of veins.

An Easter Island legend says, "The people of the Beyond have prominent veins." The statues were intended for worship of the dead, hence this representation.

Finally, we can also see in it, because of the two upraised arms, the suggestion of an incantatory attitude toward the spirits of the dead.

. The *moai* has been carved in its complete form but it is still connected to the volcano by the ridge of stone on its back, as is shown by the little line on the left side of the sign.

. Punctuation makes these two signs go together.

This sign represents the ridge on the back of the statue, connecting it to the volcano like an umbilical cord which will later be cut, freeing the statue from its original stone.

It will be placed upright at the foot of the volcano, and will remain upright forever afterward. It is turned toward its future location, with its arm thrown back. It is finished but does not yet have *mana,* since the circle has not been inscribed. It is here shown in profile; we will have occasion to return to this point, which implies one of the reasons why the statue does not bear the distinctive sign of *mana.*

. Then the double system of ropes around the

statue (which I have already described) will be put in place. It must be kept in mind that in each alternate phase of the forward motion in semicircles, one of the ropes remains fixed, serving as a guide ' , while the other imparts the rotary movement that makes the statue advance first in one direction, then in the other  .

These two symmetrical systems of ropes are independent of each other and their functions are alternately different. Their design and installation are under the control of an initiate. The initiated priest is symbolized in another part of the Tomenika manuscript that also deals with the work of the statues:  . He has long ears and bears the circle of Knowledge. He holds the system of ropes that acts as a guide in one phase and transmits motive power in the other.

. Only two initiated priests possessed *mana* for transporting statues. They are simply indicated here by two circles of initiation. The supernatural force of *mana* surrounds them like an aura.

. The statue will be animated by *mana*. It will "rise": the circle of initiation is at the top. Its weight will be "diminished": the symbol is tapered at the bottom, as though the statue had less contact with the ground.

. The statue can now go toward its *ahu*, and

this sign is quite evocative of that motion. Moreover, in its body and its motion it bears the mark of knowledge and initiation inscribed on its base, seen this time from the front and represented by a rhombus.

. These three signs are associated in a single "sentence."

The central sign is the profile of the statue with its hat . The statue is complete only when its hat has been put in place. To achieve that, the hat must be brought (right-hand sign) and lifted (left-hand sign).

. The hat will be brought by the same system of ropes used for the statue. The sign indicates the successive positions occupied by the hat in the course of its movement. To make this clearer, I will analyze the sign as follows:

+ ROPES =

Let me here state this "postulate": A *single sign* (in this case a circle) *drawn four times indicates motion of an object.*

Other considerations have led me to believe that *the object, whatever it may be, is represented by three elements.*

As we continue "reading" this writing, we will find supporting evidence for this view.

Thus an engraved or carved wooden object is represented as follows:

. That is why I say that these three rhombuses correspond to the statue.

We have already seen that on the statue in motion the lower part is drawn in a "rhombic" manner.

. Therefore the complete left-hand sign indicates that the hat (the three circles) will be lifted onto the statue (the three rhombuses) in a paricular direcion in relation to it. Taking into account certain indications of direction revealed by the position of the ideograms in this line, we are led to conclude that the hat was lifted from behind the statue, after the statue was in place on its *ahu*.

To sum up:

. Movement of transporting the statue by means of ropes.

The statue with its hat in place (seen in profile).

The statue receiving its hat, with an indication of the direction in which the hat will be lifted in relation to the statue.

. The hat will be lifted on a ramp of ropes, represented by the two vertical lines, with the four circles on the left showing the successive positions of the hat as it rises, and the three semicircles on the right showing its upward motion. The three semicircles touch the line at four places, and four is the representation of motion.

The distance covered by the hat during its ascent. Four ideograms here also, since there is motion.

The hat will move upward.

On the ramp of ropes, it will cover all the intermediate distances from the bottom to the top of its course. We will see that the concept of multiplicity is indicated by repeating a sign.

When the hat has moved all along the ramp of ropes, its ascent will be finished. Four round signs have been associated here to represent the entire upward movement.

The last sign in this line, in which Tomenika explains the mechanism of lifting the hat: by the stone winch to which it is attached.

This sign is only a representation of another, with which you are now familiar:

The little appendage added to the Easter Island ideogram clearly expresses the idea that ropes are involved.

I believe that the statue of which I have spoken was made for a king's son whose name was Ku'uku'u. We must recall the legend of the first explorers of the island.

At the court of King Hotu Matua, in Hiva, lived an oracle named Hau Maka. He dreamed, and his spirit went to Matakiterani (the ancient name of Easter Island); then he returned to Hiva and said, "There is an island in the direction of the rising sun, and you will go to live there with King Hotu Matua."

Six sons of kings, all initiates, went to explore the island and make preparations for the arrival of King Hotu Matua. With them went the spirit of Hau Maka. When they arrived at the island, they saw a turtle on the shore. It was a spirit turtle; they tried in vain to catch it. Ku'uku'u was the last to try. It struck him a violent blow with its flipper and left him for dead. He did die, and the turtle went back to Hiva.

Here, again, are the first six characters of the line:

. || . He died.

One of the lines is birth, the other is death. Between the two is life. On either side are the two infinities: before birth and after death.

. Ku'uku'u had lived. Here lies his lifeless Long-Ear body.

. This sign, beside the representation of the corpse, is so important that I will speak of it later.

. The seven explorers (six sons of kings and the spirit of Hau Maka), all initiates; there is thus the round sign. They are all of the same royal origin, "flesh of the same flesh," whose original attachment to Hiva is indicated by the two small lateral lines. At the bottom, one of the heads is not marked: the spirit of Hau Maka. At the top, one of the heads is flat: that of Ku'uku'u, which has already been drawn flat, like that of the statue which will embody him.

. His current of life, starting from Hiva, grows, reaches the apogee of youth, then begins diminishing and turning inward, tending through death to return to where life came from. But it does not return to Hiva, and the circle is not closed.

. Only the spirit turtle, here stylized without a head, returns to Hiva.

. Work was then begun on his statue, which was to see him after his earthly life was ended.

And you know the rest of that formidable line of *rongo-rongo* writing:

The symbol of the turtle is turned to the right, showing that the turtle moves toward the open sea.

The sign , however, representing the profile of the statue with its hat in place, is turned in the other direction. And we know that these statues had their backs to the sea.

It was analysis of these directions that made me say that the lifting of the hat was done from behind the statue when it was on its *ahu*.

. . No circle of initiation here. There is no need for it, because this is the sign of Knowledge itself, Knowledge of the gravest kind: that of death.

The ancient Easter Islanders saw death, beyond suffering and anguish, as a phenomenon of escape in space, with the "I" abandoning the "me," an escape that is at first small in space and slow in time, a time not measured by that of mankind's clocks, but by the time of the universe. Then this phenomenon, in itself, becomes gigantic, cosmic. The "consciousness" of the "I" moves away faster and faster, while becoming dispersed in immensity. This dispersion becomes so great, so diluted, that the movement slows down and the "consciousness" is immobilized in the black, blue, deep, dense eternity of the spatial infinity between the stars, where it experiences calm, the great calms. All this is what the sign means, in the "I's" movement of escape by death, toward an infinite of another infinite.

That is what the statues of Easter Island looked at, those that saw and had become greater and greater: those consciousnesses of the dead that are the spaces between the stars.

Matakiterani, the ancient name of Easter Island: "Eyes Looking at the Stars."

At the beginning of each new year, the birdman cult was celebrated on the Orongo cliff. The people watched for the arrival of the sea birds on the three little islands at the foot of the cliff. The man who found and brought back the first egg, after having dipped it in the sea, consecrated a new "chosen one of the god" for a year: the birdman, endowed with *mana* and given almost divine privileges. Such was the worship of life on Easter Island.

Eyeless statues felt the vibrations of space with their empty sockets, seeking the lost original continent, or received the forces of the south winds.

People in very ancient times had made unknown statues, different from all the others, statues whose inspiration came from elsewhere, far away.

And other statues looked at death.

Time has passed. We may forget the ropes that it has destroyed, and let the little children of the island play their games with string. But let us remember *mana*, for otherwise nothing would have any meaning. The stone giants still remain. We are forever limited to taking only small steps in their domain, because . . .

On the steep Orongo cliff, above a dizzying drop of a thousand feet, is an *ahu*: here were gigantic statues . . . *Mana.*

A place of knowledge of life and death.

Te Pito no te Henua, another name of Easter Island: "Navel of the World."

To which one comes and to which one will go.

CHAPTER TWO

Making the Statues

In the preceding chapter, on the basis of a line from the Tomenika manuscript, I discussed how the statues were transported, how their stone hats were lifted, and the meaning of the second-period statues consecrated to worship of the dead.

It has been said that the Easter Island ideograms were simply memory aids whose purpose was to preserve a narrative known only to initiates. Although I translated the line from right to left, there is nothing to prevent us from assuming that it could also be read in the other direction, keeping all its meaning but using another tense: the imperfect, for example, instead of the future that I used.

But we must bear in mind that the ideograms represent an elaborate and precise form of writing, even though they are neither alphabetical nor syllabic. There were schools of *rongo-rongo* writing on Easter Island. Tradition says that certain kings kept close watch over them. And so, of course, did those directly responsible for them: priests and initiates.

The second line of the Tomenika manuscript that I will consider deals with the making of the statues and the workers who took part in it. In this case it is more a matter of illustration than of narrative in the strict sense, as we will see. The narrative seems less consecutive than in the first line.

For this reason I feel it is easy to explain the misunderstanding that arose between the last Easter Island initiates and the travelers who questioned them in the hope of learning the secret of *rongorongo* writing. When one of those Easter Islanders was shown a carved tablet he related no story and simply said, "This is a birdman, this is a cock," and so on. He was called an impostor; from then on, communication was forever broken off with that man who could have made so many revelations. The tablet shown to him probably bore a number of signs that required no identifications other than those he made, since their pictorial form was enough to evoke in his mind an "immediate" interpretation of everything they implied.

But let us come back to the second line of ideograms:

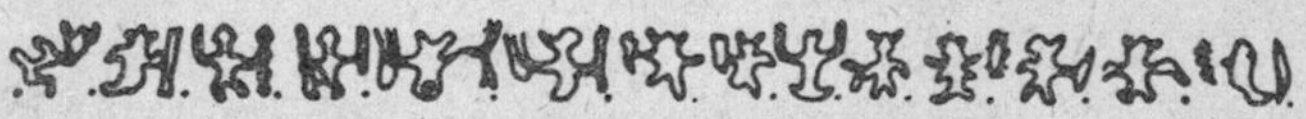

If, as I maintain, this line deals with the complete work of sculpture, the different categories of people who took part in that work must be represented in it, along with the statue itself, of course. We will see that this is the case: not only are the sculptors present, but also those who transported the statues and lifted the hats. This line is one of the few in which Short-Ears are depicted. *Rongo-rongo* writing belonged exclusively to Long-Ear initiates and they had little interest in writing about the common people.

The two signs at the ends of the line indicate that the making of statues was accompanied by specific rites: dances and a feast.

. . The last descendants of the Long-Ears told Thor Heyerdahl about the tradition that dances were performed before a statue was begun: the dancers then wore masks. Early visitors to Easter Island reported having seen dances whose movements were performed while the dancers stood or hopped on one foot. In the case we are considering, these dances were to some extent an incantation addressed to those who were "in the sky," and also to those whose spirits had rejoined the original land of Hiva, for, as we will see, that is the meaning which follows from the orientation of the sign to the right.

. . The sign at the other end of the line indicates that a feast was given. This symbol corresponds to the Easter Island *umu*, a kind of underground oven in which food–fish in this case–was cooked on heated stones. The whole oven was covered with leaves, then opened when cooking was completed.

leaves fish stone

. . A sculptor. In agreement with tradition, it

is clearly shown here that the Long-Ears themselves sculptured the stone giants of Rano Raraku.

. . Going from right to left, the next sign deserves our attention. It seems to show that the sculptor received his tool—here a stone axe—from the birdman, whom we discover here for the first time. Why?

On the one hand, it was possession of those tools—axes, gravers, knives and others—that made it possible to develop that statuary. On the other hand, the birdman embodied the god of the island, Make-Make, and received *mana*. The Easter Islanders regarded those stone tools as a divine gift. To illustrate this, the sculptor is shown receiving his tool from an embodiment of the divinity: the birdman.

But the presence of the birdman giving a stone axe further implies that inspiration for the sculpture also came from the god Make-Make.

The birdman cult died out in the middle of the nineteenth century. It was probably as old as the expansion of the Easter Island statuary. Two reasons make me inclined to believe this:

—If the statues were connected with worship of the dead and death, there was almost necessarily an equivalent worship of life, like the birdman cult, which we will discuss in detail later.

—More important, the birdman is often represented on the wooden tablets, which are much older than the Tomenika manuscript.

. . Heyerdahl also reports the tradition that the sculptors wore fern crowns while they worked.

This Long-Ear woman has gathered ferns and made them into a crown which she will give to the sculptor. It is known that Easter Island women wore skirts made from fibers of the bark of the paper mulberry tree.

. The master sculptor, who will outline the future statue by making regularly spaced holes in the stone, using a knife. Such holes can still be seen on unfinished statues.

He seems to be holding a square. This indicates the regular spacing of the holes. Actually, however, one has the impression that the unit of measurement he used was the length of his forearm. After making the first hole with a pointed tool, he put his elbow over it, made another hole, put his elbow over that one, and so on.

Since it was he who outlined the statue on the stone, it is natural that the following sign should be a representation of the completed statue.

. The entire statue. As in all signs depicting a statue, the head is flat. The arms and hands (which were actually placed over the stomach, with long, tapering fingernails, at least in statues of the first period) are here shown upraised, revealing the incantatory nature of those statues with regard to the realm of the dead.

Let us recall the sign of which I said that it suggests the preliminary outlining of the statue. There is little difference between the two; we have only to imagine the head and the lower part, which

I will indicate by dotted lines, to make them essentially identical:

Finally, let us consider the convex base of the statue. In the method of transporting the statues that I have described, this shape would facilitate their forward motion, upright and turning in semicircles, by means of the system of ropes, because friction between the ground and the base of the statue would be greatly reduced. And the statues of the second period did in fact have slightly convex bases.

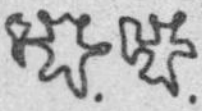

. . . Two Long-Ear sculptors at work. One detail is striking: each of them seems to have one leg shorter than the other. This is to show that they are sculpting, in a natural and understandable position. Work was done on both sides of the statue by means of two access passages. The sculptors put one knee against it, and so they had one leg bent.

. 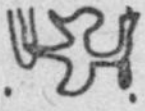 . The form of this sign alone shows us the birdman. From his left arm hangs the scarf of tapa (bark cloth) that he carried as a distinctive emblem.

But the second meaning of the sign is of great importance. It is the birdman, endowed with divinity, who will transmit to the initiated priest, to his left in this line, the inspiration for the system of ropes used in transporting the statues. The symbol illustrating this method of transportation is .  . (see Chapter 1). Examining the sign of the birdman, we see that what he holds in his right hand corresponds to this part of the preceding ideogram , while his

left arm and the tapa scarf are similar to this

part of the complete sign . .

We may conclude that in the minds of the ancient Easter Islanders the method of transporting the statues was of a divine essence and had been inspired by the god Make-Make through his human incarnation, the birdman.

The initiated priest, with the long ears characteristic of the noble class, bearing the circle of Knowledge, has received from the birdman the inspiration for the method of transporting the statues. In one hand he holds the system of ropes that serves as

a guide and in the other the system that transmits

the motive power as I explained in the first chapter.

. . . Finally, two Short-Ears. Unlike all the human figures we have seen so far, these are shown without ears.

. . One of them is a worker whose task is to lift the hats by means of the stone winch he symbolically holds in one hand. He is standing at the foot of the rope ramp stretched over the top of the statue to support the winch and the hat attached to it.

. The other Short-Ear works in transporting the statue. It is here represented by four rhombuses which, as we have seen, imply the idea of motion.

To show that three rhombuses are the object, in this case the statue, and that four represents its motion, I will offer the following illustration. Let us move the "object" in the direction of the arrow, with the distance traveled being equal to the length of one of the elements composing it:

=

Let us now superimpose the two signs. The resulting sign consists of four rhombuses.

. The concept and installation of the winch, however, belong exclusively to the Long-Ears.

We have now seen all those who, through the ages, belonged to the Easter Island civilization which flowered in that gigantic, grandiose work and then vanished into the shadow of its statues.

CHAPTER THREE

Birth of a Child

We have examined two lines of ideograms dealing with statues consecrated to worship of the dead. It is natural to assume that, along with these lines referring to death, there must also have been some reference to life. This is confirmed by the following line in the Tomenika manuscript, which concerns the birth of a child and the various events that accompanied it in ancient Easter Island society, whose memory has been preserved by tradition.

For convenience of presentation I will read this line from right to left.

This first sign is a symbol of fecundation. It bears the circle because it is charged with *mana*.

At first the sign which surmounts it and is connected to it made me think of an obsidian blade, and

I believed it indicated that the Easter Islanders were acquainted with the female reproductive system either because they already practiced Caesarean sections, which is only a hypothesis, or because they performed human sacrifices, which is known.

Besides this interpretation, however, there is another, related to the tradition reported to Francis Mazière by Gabriel Veriveri, the last initiate: "For a man to know when he should couple with a woman, he must watch during the first eight days of the new moon, Mahinau-o'hua, the moon of the penis. He must find the woman and couple with her. The child born of this union, a perfect child, is worthy of being seen. These are the children who will be recommended for the *rongo-rongo* learning, for the cult of the birdman . . ."

I will therefore say that the sign represents the pregnant uterus, a single Fallopian tube (women usually have only one child at a time) which is connected to this symbol above the uterus to indicate that impregnation took place during the new moon

. A representation of the contents of the pregnant uterus, "united in all parts to the mother," and of the umbilical cord and the placenta.

. A diagram of the flow of blood from the mother's heart to the child. We will later see a complete form of this diagram.

. 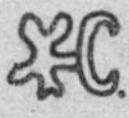 . The priest who will tie the umbilical cord. Since he does not bear the circle of Knowledge, one might think that he was a low-ranking priest assigned to perform that function which, though important to the Easter Islanders, was nevertheless quite common. That is not the case, however, because he has very large ears, a distinctive sign of the noble, dominant class, and of his high rank.

In his hand he holds the emblem of his function: the umbilical cord which he will tie and cut. He appears early in the account related by this line of ideograms because, as Alfred Métraux reports, his function actually began before childbirth, and the dreams he had during the preceding night oriented the child's later life.

The dreams of priests often appear in Easter Island traditions. Each year, for example, the name of the man who was to become the birdman was seen in dreams by the priests.

.  . An extraordinary symbol. Long before the circulation of the blood was described by Harvey, Easter Island writing showed the flow of blood from the mother's heart (where we clearly see the aorta, the trunk and the two branches of the pulmonary artery; that is enough to indicate the flow of blood to and from the heart) to the pregnant uterus and the fetus, which appears in the following sign.

.  . The fetus, connected to the umbilical cord.

.  . The tying of the umbilical cord was accompanied by a precise rite that was highly important to the child.

This act had a particular meaning: the way of tying the cord conditioned the *mana* contained in the child's body and received from his parents. Traditions are numerous and unanimous on this subject: *it was the head that received and bore* mana.

We should therefore not be surprised to see the sign which schematically illustrates this important point:

head	head and umbilical cord 	tying of the cord on the side of the child 	tying of the cord on the side of the placenta 

The next three ideograms . . . precisely indicate how the cord was tied.

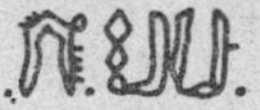

. . Overall diagram of the ligatures.
Five ligatures on the side of the child  .

Three on the side of the placenta  .

I have put an arrow at the place where the cord was cut. The priest cut it with his teeth; no obsidian tool was ever used.

In the preceding sign , the side of the child is indicated as follows:  , with the loop close to the head. The other part  therefore indicates the side of the placenta.

To summarize:

Side of the placenta . . Side of the child

Under those conditions, these two signs . . not separated by punctuation, become quite explicit. The arrows mark the locations of the ligatures:

Five ligatures on the side of the child.

Three ligatures on the side of the placenta.

In this last sign the small lateral line indicates the side connected to the mother. There is no ligature on the upper-right-hand side because the cord is still connected to the placenta before delivery.

With regard to that small lateral line, let us recall a similar one in the sign indicating the statue that has been completed but is still connected to the volcano by the ridge on its back , as by an umbilical cord . (See Chapter 1.)

Finally, on the subject of those three and five ligatures, let us note something which may not be merely a coincidence:

"In the third and fifth months of pregnancy," writes Alfred Métraux, "an important ceremony took place. In the course of it, the father-in-law gave his daughter-in-law the gift of a meal cooked in an *umu* known as the 'ceremonial chicken-intestines oven.' The meal was composed of a choice food, a chicken intestine, to honor the future child."

The sign indicating a chicken intestine follows immediately. It must be pointed out that a chicken intestine was the only food the mother ate after delivery.

Here is the chicken, holding an egg. As we have already seen with regard to the birdman cult, the egg was a symbol of new life. Let us note in passing that the same thing was done with the umbilical cord as with the egg found by the birdman's servant: they were both—the egg after a year, the cord immediately after birth—either thrown into the sea or hidden in a rocky hollow.

Let us stop a moment, because there seems to be something abnormal here. Easter Island traditions and legends, as they have been reported to us, speak of a chicken intestine. A mistake must have been made in interpreting or translating them. It was not made by the Easter Islanders themselves. Except for rats, chickens were the only animals that lived on their island, and they constantly ate them. Since they were careful observers of nature, they could not have failed to be thoroughly acquainted with the anatomy of the chicken.

A chicken intestine, full of stones or bile, is not edible. Furthermore, there can be no symbolic relation between the intestine and pregnancy.

We can only conclude that, contrary to all reports, the intestine was not involved. Next to a hen's intestine is a tube about a foot long, known as the oviduct. It is tapered at the upper end near the ovary and it widens at the lower part, from which the egg emerges.

It has exactly this shape: .

It is said to be very good to eat, and is highly appreciated as a food in some French provinces.

The symbolic connection between the oviduct and pregnancy is obvious. The mother ate an oviduct in order to favor the proper development of her pregnancy. By an extension of meaning, as we will see later, the oviduct was identified with the umbilical cord.

In the preceding pages, to make the translation of the ideograms become accurate, "chicken intestine" must be replaced by "oviduct."

The mother ate an oviduct at two periods of her pregnancy: the third and fifth months.

It is known that even numbers were considered unlucky by the Easter Islanders; the number of statues on an *ahu*, for example, is nearly always odd. But other arguments can be used to explain these periods. When Francis Mazière discovered in a cave a basalt statue, unique in its style, representing a squatting woman giving birth (a photograph of it appears in his book *Mysteries of Easter Island*), he noted that there had been veritable "delivery rooms" on the island. We must assume that all the phases of gestation were well known to the ancient Easter Islanders, who had observed them in interruptions of pregnancy for various reasons. These periods correspond to anatomical realities with amazing precision:

—By the end of the third month, embryogenesis is completed.

—By the end of the fifth month, the child is completely formed. (In our time, with the means at our disposal, a child can be considered viable at this stage of development.)

I will here end this long digression and pick up the thread of the narrative revealed in the writing.

. After birth, the father heated stones which were applied to the mother's belly to facilitate delivery of the afterbirth, as reported by Métraux.

. . Another extraordinary ideogram. The child is born, and that newcomer to life will embody the forces of the universe, in perpetual movement and repetition, here symbolized by a known sign: the swastika. But the upper part seems oriented in the opposite direction from the three other branches. This is not surprising, since it is characteristic of the "philosophy" of Easter Island: the upper part, the "head" of the symbol, is oriented toward Hiva, the original land from which came Hotu Matua, the first king of the island. We have already seen other signs turned toward the right which, by that orientation, indicate the direction of Hiva (see Chapter 1).

. . A representation of the first seven explorers who came from Hiva to make preparations for Hotu Matua's arrival. The two small lines on the upper part, which indicate their filial attachment to Hiva, are turned toward the right.

.  . It is the same with the spirit turtle which they met on the beach when they arrived and which, according to legend, returned to Hiva.

.  . The last ideograms in the line. When the mother had given birth, Métraux tells us, the priest received the offering of a cock that could not be killed without destroying the child's *mana*. Here is the cock, and the sign next to him indicates his crowing. Carved on the wall of a cave on the little island of Motu Nui, there is a bird with a long ribbon coming from his beak, representing his singing. This cock is turned toward Hiva. His crowing will carry across the sea the news that a child has been born on Easter Island.

In some cases, what happened at birth also happened at death: legend says that when King Hotu Matua felt that he was about to die he climbed to the top of the volcano, turned toward Hiva and said, "Make the cock crow."

Here, the sign depicting the cock crowing to announce the birth of a child combines the ribbon mentioned above and the silhouette of the child, with a summary outline of his head and limbs  .

.  . In the sign of death by escape of the "I" (see Chapter 1), the upraised arms evoke a flight into space.

.  . In the sign of life, one orientation is given by the "head" turned toward Hiva, and another by the downturned "arm," stressing the link with the earth.

Te Pito no te Henua: "Navel of the World."
The place of knowledge of life and death.

Symbol of death:

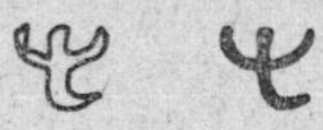

Symbol of life:

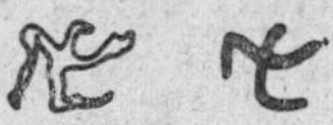

Between these two signs, identical and opposite, the wheel of time turns only one cycle. But in what dimension?

CHAPTER FOUR
The Birdman Cult

The birdman cult was such an important and distinctive part of the Easter Islanders' religious life that it could not fail to be fully depicted in *rongo-rongo* writing. We will examine the line in the Tomenika manuscript that illustrates it.

First, on the basis of the account given by Alfred Métraux, I will summarize the meaning and form of the ceremony.

Legend says that the god Make-Make brought the sea birds with him, to give them a shelter. After a long voyage he led them to the little islands at the foot of the Orongo cliff: Motu Nui, Motu Iti and Motu Kao-Kao, which is only a rocky spur.

For Easter Islanders the sea swallow, *manu tara*, became an incarnation of the god Make-Make, and the first egg laid each spring symbolized the return of new life. Possession of that egg consecrated the birdman, the *tangata manu,* who would be inhabited by the god.

Each year the same ceremony took place, and each year a new birdman was named. He had great privileges but he also had obligations: he had to live in seclusion and remain continent, under penalty of death. His hand, which had touched the egg, could not come in contact with food; he therefore needed a servant. Being a human incarnation of Make-Make, he of course possessed the mystical force of *mana.* In *rongo-rongo* writing the sign for the birdman, represented in various attitudes and forms, does not bear the circle of *mana.* That is quite understandable, since the birdman was an embodiment of divine power; a representation of him clearly evoked it, with no need of an additional symbol.

Here, as an example, is a symbol of the birdman that we saw in Chapter 2, where I pointed out that he transmitted to an initiated priest the inspiration for the method of transporting the statues. The symbol depicts the long tapa scarf that he carried on his arm after being consecrated.

Each spring, those who sought the title of birdman (those whose names had been seen in dreams by the priests), along with their families and tribes, went up and settled in the stone houses of Orongo village, on the ridge of the volcano that overlooks the crater on one side and the sea on the other. Each candidate appointed a servant, called a *hopu manu,* who had to climb down the cliff and swim across the shark-infested channel to the little island of Motu Nui. There, hidden in a small cave, he would watch the sea birds flying and try to find the first-laid egg for his master.

The long wait began, marked by continuous ceremonies at Orongo and constant watching of the sea birds by the *hopu manus* on the island of Motu Nui. At last came the day when the first egg was found. The *hopu manu* who had discovered it put it in the place on the island called the "bird's cry," and from there he shouted his master's name to the cliff, followed by the words, "You, shave your head." For the birdman had to shave off all the hair on his head, including his eyebrows and eyelashes, probably in order to be as smooth as an egg. The name of the new birdman was transmitted to the population by a watcher who had stayed in a cave, called "listening to the bird," in the face of the Orongo cliff.

On the island of Motu Nui, the *hopu manu* made the highly significant gesture of dipping the egg into the sea. Had life come from the sea? He then tied it to his forehead with a tapa ribbon and, accompanied by the other *hopu manus*, swam back to Orongo. He climbed the cliff and gave his master that egg charged with magic and divine forces.

The birdman received the egg with his outstretched hand covered by a tapa scarf in which a piece of sandalwood, said to have been brought by Hotu Matua, was inserted. He went into a trance, as though suddenly inhabited by the god. He then led all the people in a procession down to the village of Mataveri, where there were ceremonies with human sacrifices to the god Make-Make.

Here is the line of ideograms illustrating this cult:

The account is centered on the channel. . separating the cliff from the island of Motu Nui. For the sake of precision, and because the signs are separated by punctuation, I will say that this one . . indicates the sea and this one . . indicates the channel between Orongo and Motu Nui. As we will see, the distinction is important because this set of signs, as it is placed in the line, must have these two meanings. It also has a third meaning which will appear later.

We will consider the ideograms without apparent order. In our language and with our concepts, it would be difficult to follow the narrative from left to right or right to left without many grammatical acrobatics. But we will easily see how everything becomes clear and explicit, as though the signs spoke for themselves, once all the phases of the birdman rite are known.

. Each year, in spring, when seeds sprout and the first leaves appear,

then when flowers blossom

. and the first sea swallows arrive (a curious detail: the whole sign evokes the sea swallow, but the rear part already prefigures the silhouette of the birdman's head),

. beyond the shark-infested channel separating the cliffs from the islands

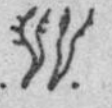

. are the two islands of Motu Nui and Motu Iti, still covered with the ancient grass of Easter Island, where the sea birds come to lay their eggs.

. That is where the *hopu manus* had to swim (the left-hand figure represents a swimming *hopu manu*, seen from above, and beside him is the pointed float made of *totora* reeds in which he brought provisions for his long wait on the island)

. in order to look for the first-laid egg.

Later the egg was emptied, filled with tapa and hung for a year in the hut occupied by the birdman near the Rano Raraku volcano.

The oblique line also indicates the opening of hatching, if it had taken place.

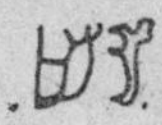

. To show that the egg contains new life, the embryo is on the left, and on the right is the sea swallow chick that it will become.

In the line dealing with the birth of a child, we saw that the fetus was represented by this sign: .

I have redrawn the bird embryo to show the resemblance between the two signs.

. This symbol associates the egg with the oviduct. The meaning of the latter is extended to take on that of "umbilical cord." We can thus state the two meanings of the ideogram:

—The egg and the umbilical cord are symbols of new life and, more precisely, of the means by which that life arrives.

—Moreover, they both had the same fate on Easter Island: the birdman's egg, at the end of a year, and the umbilical cord, immediately after birth, were either thrown into the sea or hidden in a rocky hollow.

We have now reached the crucial moment of this religious drama. The first egg has been found. The *hopu manu* who has taken possession of it is about to go to the part of the little island known as the "bird's cry," from where he will shout his master's name.

. 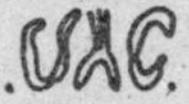 . Here is the "bird's cry."

This long ribbon represents the cry itself: "You, shave your head," preceded by the name of the man who will become the birdman.

We have already seen a similar sign in Chapter 3:  ., the crowing of the cock announcing the birth of a child.

The *hopu manu*'s hand and arm, with fingers joined and thumb extended, about to be raised to his mouth to amplify his voice.

Another representation of the same gesture: the hand cupped beside the mouth.

. The same sign, but with a line through it. Is this meant to indicate that the *hopu manu* cupped both hands around his mouth to shout? Or does it simply mean that Tomenika made a mistake and crossed out this sign because it duplicated the one next to it? That is a likely assumption.

. This shout, announcing the name of the new birdman, will cross the channel between Motu Nui and the Orongo cliff . . . ... at Orongo, where there was a sacred statue. One highly unusual feature of this sign in that the statue seems to be facing the sea. It does not bear the circle of *mana* because it is shown in profile; we will examine that point later.

I believe it is the famous statue, improperly called the "Wave Breaker," discovered in a stone house in the Orongo village and now in the British Museum.

Let us recall the representation of another statue which, although seen from the front, has the same convex base and the same flat head: . .

. In the cave known as "listening to the bird," in the face of the Orongo cliff, a watcher will hear the name of the new birdman.

Cave in the face of the cliff.

Watcher.

Symbol of the sound that he will hear when the *hopu manu* shouts the name of his master.

Let us note this similarity in passing: three signs are combined for the "bird's cry," and three for "listening to the bird."

The "bird's cry."

"Listening to the bird."

The new birdman has been named. On his outstretched hand . . covered with a tapa scarf in which a piece of sandalwood has been inserted (let us remember this representation of wood because we will encounter it later) he will receive the egg that consecrates him.

The birdman, in trance and inhabited by the god, leads the procession down to Mataveri, where other ceremonies will take place.

The same rites were performed every year. When a birdman died, he was buried in a special *ahu*, the *ahu orohie,* near the Rano Raraku volcano. Tradition required that ten cocks be attached to the dead man's toes, as may have been done with King Hotu Matua.

At the end of the translation it clearly appears that there is order and balance in this writing.

On each side of the central ideograms . . . . which indicate where the action takes place, seven groups of signs are marked off by punctuation. Quite logically, the narrative situates the facts in space, according to the place where they occur in relation to the central sign, and in time, from left to right.

CHAPTER FIVE

The *Moai Kava-Kava* Statuary

Another subject of great importance in the religious concepts of Easter Island is the development of the little wooden statues representing individuals with hollow bellies and bony chests. They are known as the *moai kava-kava* statuary.

These statuettes had supernatural power and the Easter Islanders carefully kept them in their houses, wrapped in tapa scarves. They took them out for religious ceremonies, and it has been reported that on those occasions they took them in their arms and danced with them. The statuettes were also taken out before harvests, to place the latter under a good omen.

According to a legend reported by Alfred Métraux, the origin of the statuary is as follows:

Here are the circumstances in which Chief Tuu Ko Ihu, who is to some extent the civilizing hero of Easter Island, had the idea of carving the statuettes.

He was on his way to his house of Harekoka at Hangahahave. As he was passing the hill, he saw two spirits sleeping at the foot of a section of red rock. He had time to see their ribs and hollow bellies. When he arrived at his house he took two pieces of wood and carved them to resemble the spirits he had seen. The news spread all over the island that Tuu Ko Ihu had carved wooden statues.

In the above paragraph I have given only a partial summary of Métraux's account because certain details do not coincide with what is written in the line of the Tomenika manuscript dealing with the *moai kavakava* statuary.

In the manuscript, this line immediately follows the four we have already seen. Since it concerns the origin of a work of art, translation of it necessarily involves certain abstract ideas. For that reason, the ideograms should be considered in the special order I will propose.

Here is the story of that statuary:

. Tuu Ko Ihu, who bears the circle of initiation, saw two demons, here shown on either side of him.

. Tuu Ko Ihu.

. One of the demons, leaning against a section of rock.

. The other demon.

.  . He walked away. In his mind arose the idea of representing the two demons united, complementing each other.

It is strange to note that if their figures are drawn with a single line and then superimposed, we find the swastika :  . One of the demons only has to be turned in relation to the other. This may seem artificial, but we will see at the end of the line that it is what Tuu Ko Ihu did.

. He imagined them indissolubly linked and decided to carve them together.

.  . He took a stone axe and cut down a tree (the statuettes were made from the trunk of the *toro miro* tree).

Tuu Ko Ihu is here represented in the guise of the birdman, showing the divine nature attributed to him by legend and the scribe.

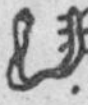

. _ _ _ _ _ .  . An important point: to stress the fact that this statuary came from wood, the sign indicating the roots of the tree is at one end of the line, while those indicating the trunk and the foliage, not separated by punctuation, are at the other end, framing the whole legend:

roots:  trunk  foliage:

.  To stress again that the statuary had its origin in the tree, this piece of wood is shown connected to an umbilical cord or an oviduct, taken in the meaning of "means by which life arrives."

. . Let us recall the egg and the umbilical cord in Chapter 4.

Here we have . . Meaning: The life of this mode of artistic expression comes from wood.

. . This sign schematically illustrates what Tuu Ko Ihu decided to carve: a *moai kava-kava*. It is expressed here by one of the string figures with which the ancient Easter Islanders were familiar. The three loops are enough to individualize the head, the trunk and the limbs.

. . The neighboring signs show that with a tool he carved the wood to give it three parts: head, trunk, limbs.

In the chapter on the birdman cult we saw this sign for a piece of sandalwood: . It is similar to the preceding sign and has the meaning of "carved wood."

. Tuu Ko Ihu took the knotty trunk of the tree. He carved each end of it according to his memory of the demons he had briefly seen.

. . When he had finished his work, he cut away the wood between the two ends: the two demons were there. They have only to be opposed, by turning the one on the left, to obtain the representation of

each one as it is inscribed in this line: .

. One of the demons.

. The other, with his forked head which through the work of the artist, recalls the initial

vision: .

Through five consecutive lines on one page of the unique Tomenika manuscript, we have seen five fundamental aspects of the life of the Easter Islanders:

—The birdman cult.

—Transportation of the statues and lifting of the hats.

—The "artisans" who took part in erecting the statues of the second period.

—The birth of a child.

—The origin of the *moai kava-kava* statuary.

CHAPTER SIX

Transporting the Statues

We are now going to examine another line of ideograms: the third from the top on another page of the Tomenika manuscript, reproduced in the photographic section of this book.

This line again deals with transporting a statue intended to reach a particular place (the *ahu*) and stand in a particular position (facing away from the sea).

At the end of the translation we will find a highly important indication that may contain the key to one of the most crucial problems of Easter Island.

First I will briefly summarize the method of transporting the statues:

Rope on one side. *Rope on the other side.*

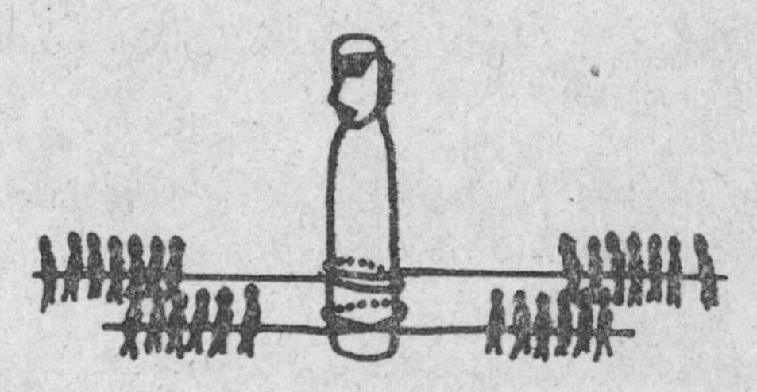

Double system of ropes.

The two teams of men in front of the statue alternately make it move forward in a semicircle. There are two teams on each rope: those in front make the statue move forward, those in back keep the rope taut to maintain the balance of the statue and prevent it from slipping.

Seen from above, the system can be depicted as follows, with the black disk representing the statue:

One side.

The other side.

The two ropes around the statue thus move it in this pattern: . The vertical arrow shows the direction of forward motion; the other two arrows show the semicircular motion, first in one direction, then in the other.

The sign designating the ropes used in transporting the statues is already known to us from the first chapter: .

We will read this line from right to left:

. Installation of the double system of ropes making it possible to move the statue forward in semicircles:

A set of ropes and a carved wooden stick. These are the emblems of one of the two initiated priests whose *mana* made the statue move (we will later see the sign of the two priests themselves).

With regard to the carved wooden stick , whose three parts made it comparable to the sign in Chapter 4, many Easter Island traditions say that each priest held a long stick covered with *rongo-rongo* signs. Let us recall the image of the initiated priest as we saw it in Chapter 2: . . In one hand he holds a set of ropes . Let us imagine that in his other hand he holds the sacerdotal stick

With these two elements . we now have a representation of the initiated priest possessing *mana*.

Then comes this long succession of geometrical shapes in which we see that one sign, can participate in the elaboration of several ideas.

The unwinding of a complete turn of the rope making the statue move a distance twice as great as the diameter of its base.

On each side of the statue several ropes were wound around it, one above another.

Four separate teams of men were necessary for transporting a statue.

. With each semicircle forward, the distance covered by the statue doubled, tripled, etc.

It is interesting to note that our "etc." was written as by the Easter Islanders, showing that the same process could be continued indefinitely.

Similarly, the statue, here shown as , is not "closed" at the top; the process of transporting it remained the same, whatever its height.

On each side of the statue, as many ropes as were needed to transport it were placed on top of each other.

. . Legend is specific on this point: only two priests possessed the *mana* needed for transporting the statues. Those two priests are here, like two auras charged with *mana*.

Each of them bears two circles representing *mana*, to show that each communicated that supernatural force to the two teams of men, both holding the ropes on one side of the statue, who were under his authority.

. . On the left, a symbol of the object in this case the statue. On the right, a symbol of the movement of the statue, , with the ropes barely sketched. We have already encountered this idea in Chapter 1: that three elements designate an object and that four of the same elements designate its movement.

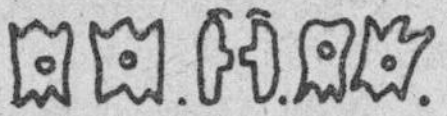

These six signs must be divided into two parts.

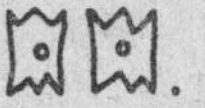

The teams of men seem to receive the *mana* with which they are marked here. It will give them the extraordinary strength to move the statue. In the method of transporting the statues by a double system of ropes, only one team is pulling forward at any given time. The *rongo-rongo* writing clearly indicates this: in the representation of the four teams, one of them is different, showing this forward pulling  , while the other on the same side shows a backward pulling  to keep the rope taut.

During a semicircular movement, the two teams on the other side do not move. They are shown as identical: ..

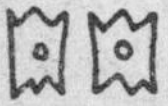

. The statue moves forward in semicircles, first in one direction, then in the other, on its convex base.

We will recall the entire statue  , in which the base is represented as: .

The two small lines indicate the movement of rotation in alternating directions; hence the sign .. to depict that mode of forward progression.

. . No drawing could have given a better representation of the men pulling the statue than this figure taken from the game of strings.

. . These two signs, not separated by punctuation, indicate that the statue has at least been brought to its final location.

It is here seen from the front, to show the circle of *mana* inscribed on it.

Here it is seen in profile, for it will face away from the sea. (We have already seen the Orongo statue in profile; the similarity is obvious.)

On the other side of the sea, toward which the statue will turn its back . . , is this sign . , so big that the scribe had to "curve" it to make it have the same height as the others. He also placed it "on the other side of the sea," as an indication of origin. *For this sign, and it alone in all the Easter Island writing, is the symbol of Hiva, the land that was the starting point of the Polynesian migration led by King Hotu Matua.*

Let sailors and travelers look at it closely. If they remember having seen a monument like a big totem pole somewhere in the Pacific, and if this sign reminds them of it, the place where they saw it may be the land from which Hotu Matua and his people set off on the long voyage that took them to Easter Island, as Hau Maka's dream had predicted.

But Hiva may have disappeared, as would seem to be indicated by a passage in the legend of Hotu Matua concerning the reason for his departure: "Feeling the land sinking into the sea, the king decided to leave Hiva."

My initial hypothesis on the transportation of the statues led me to conclude that ropes were used. I then referred to the ancient grass of Easter Island, which had a suitable texture for making ropes. But we know that the ancient Easter Islanders had a tree, the paper mulberry tree, from whose bark they could make cloth, fishnets and ropes. Grass must have been used also, but was it used alone? What does the writing say? Perhaps we will find an answer to this question in another line of the manuscript, immediately below the one we have just examined.

For the Easter Islanders the method of transporting the statues had a divine essence, and we have seen the birdman transmitting the inspiration for it to the initiated priest (Chapter 2):

But Tomenika implies that an initiate may have conceived a similar system, by analogy, taking his inspiration from objects of everyday life. We will read this line in a special way because it involves types of reasoning that are not always the same as those in the preceding lines, insofar as it is more constructive than figurative.

Two things can be moved forward by rotation in a manner applicable to the statues. First, a vase with a circular cross section, like the one depicted at the right-hand end of the line . , seen once from the side and once from above. Second, a top, which was the favorite toy of Easter Island children. It is depicted as follows: . Its image would be more familiar to us if it were seen horizontally: .

A vase and a top can move forward while turning, like a statue. Tomenika fuses these three objects because of this property they have in common, and we again see the base of the statue with which we are familiar. After the initial rotation has been imparted to them, all three can move forward: . .

There are two signs to illustrate this forward motion because, as we will see, the concept of multiplicity can be expressed by the repetition of a single sign. The two signs therefore indicate all objects to which the same principle can be applied, and not only the three I have mentioned. These signs are not closed at the bottom, which means that the progression can be continued indefinitely, by repeating the initial movement. This is another version of the "etc." that I pointed out in the preceding line.

The top is made of wood. Let us note in passing that the sign for it closely resembles the sign for forward motion in semicircles  (Chapter 1).

Wood comes from the tree  , here seen in its entirety, with its roots, trunk and foliage.

In Chapter 5, on the origin of the wooden statuettes, we saw that the tree was divided into its parts:

roots  trunk  foliage

The top is made of wood, like the *moai kava-kava,* simply depicted by this sign 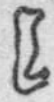 , which was more explicit in Chapter 5.

These three indivisible signs for wood .  . are not separated by punctuation.

We know, however, that four signs linked together express movement. Here we have :. 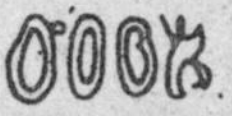 .

A man  throws a top  and makes it spin  . (The signs for circular motion and the top  have a curved line in common, which I have here emphasized by making it thicker.)

These ideograms  associated with these two  in the same sentence indicate motion, by the association of four signs.

By its shape, the sign for the man throwing the top has a specific meaning: he is going to transmit something. We will see later that the man who transmits writing is indicated as follows:  . The shapes and gestures are similar.

The man  who spins the top will transmit inspiration to an initiate who is on the other side of these signs; this initiate bears the circle of *mana*:
.

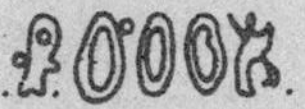

The mark of *mana* is on the upper part of the sign  .

We have already encountered a similar sign in Chapter 1,  , "The statue will be animated by *mana*; it will 'rise' and its weight will be 'diminished.'"

The location of the circle on the initiate designates him as the one who thought of transporting the statues in that way.

This initiate  had the idea of associating the motion of the top with a rope, seen here in cross section, as is indicated in the fourth sign 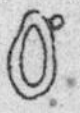 .

He conceived the application of this principle to the statues, and his arm is represented only by the cross section of the rope  which he holds out

toward the statue  .

This sign, in three parts, corresponds to a statue.

We will see another statue like it in Chapter 10:  .

But in this case the statue  is from the first period, because its base is tapered. It had not been designed for being transported and was to remain at the foot of the volcano.

The principle of transportation had to be applied to a statue from the second period with an untapered

base  , here shown with its bottom open to indicate that the system of transportation was the same, no matter what the height of the statue.

The top  came from wood  . The initiate  who had the idea of imparting a turning motion  by means of a rope would also take that rope from wood.

He cut down a tree ., on whose trunk the superimposition of ropes is already indicated, as it was indicated for the transportation of the statue at the beginning of this chapter.

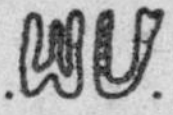

From the bark of the tree he made ropes . . .
Since they were meant to transmit movement, Tomenika depicted them by four signs.

We will see in Chapter 13 that the ancestors were involved by means of knotted cords, known as genealogical cords, depicted in writing as follows: . The Polynesians touched the knots like the beads of a rosary, and each of them represented an ancestor.

These statues were meant for ancestor worship .
The transportation, and therefore the movement, of the stone figure depicted as an ancestor is expressed by the same sign, but with four parts .
Then we again find what we already know from the preceding line:

Four groups of men were necessary for transporting a statue, whose forward motion always took place in accordance with the same principle, no matter what the distance.

Several ropes were superimposed on each side of the statue. Here we see two, and we find this mode of expression whenever the idea of multiplicity is expressed.

Each rope was wrapped around the statue once. This calls for explanation:

As we can see, in this system the rope passes once over one side of the statue and twice over the other.

The ideogram indicates this by showing two concentric circles for each rope on one side of the statue.

Finally, since a vase can be given motion like that by which a statue is transported, the statue can be represented in the same way at the other end of the line, but of course it will bear the specific mark of *mana*, the circle.

The line can now be read without difficulty from one end to the other, from right to left.

Several things should be pointed out, however. I will have occasion to stress the importance, in the Tomenika manuscript, of the two end signs of a line. In the line we have just translated, we see:

Aside from the movement of the statue, which, like the vase, has a circular base and can be given the same forward motion by rotation, the meaning that clearly appears is that the statue, like a vase, will be a receptacle for *mana.*

One question immediately arises. Since no pottery of any kind has been found on Easter Island, we may wonder if that representation of a vase was not introduced into *rongo-rongo* writing after the arrival of the first Europeans.

But there is another possibility: perhaps the vase was a memory from earlier times. Was there pottery, including vases, in Hiva, the original homeland of the Easter Islanders? There is reason to think so, since it was in Hiva that Chinese writing influenced the *rongo-rongo* signs. In ancient Chinese writing a vase was designated by the same sign that we have seen at the right-hand end of the preceding line:

Easter Island

China

To conclude this chapter, the following question should be raised: In the world of the Easter Islanders, is it conceivable that an initiate could have found his inspiration outside a strictly mystical context? To think so would amount to applying our own viewpoint to Easter Island civilization, and that would obviously be a mistake. The writing shows us that the initiate's form of thought is closely bound up with a principle that comes from the divine, even if a practical application is derived from it. The sign  representing the initiate who conceived the method of transporting the statues by analogy with other objects shows a resemblance of form, at least in its lower part, with two other signs. First, the god with the terrible face  (see Chapter 7), who was probably Make-Make. Second, the cock  (see Chapter 3), which is not surprising, since Make-Make was the god of birds.

With these considerations in mind we may conclude that Tomenika wanted to show that on Easter Island the application of certain principles should not be removed from a mystical framework even if their consequences were only material and practical.

CHAPTER SEVEN

The Genealogical Songs

I must now give a key that will enable us to decipher other lines. But since the original legends in this domain have come down to us only in a distorted and incomplete form, I do not think we can go very far in that research at present.

Here are the facts. I will borrow them from Alfred Métraux, occasionally quoting from his book *Ile de Pâques.*

The Polynesians attached great importance to genealogies. Any special occasion was a pretext for reciting a complete list of their ancestors. "The gods themselves had pedigrees and were presented as the product of a long series of unions between imaginary beings. This proclivity was also extended to nature: plants, minerals and animals had parents attributed to them."

In 1886 an American, Paymaster Thomson, learned one of these genealogical songs from an old Easter Islander named Ure Vaeiko. Thomson presented it as being the text of a *rongo-rongo* tablet.

"Thomson's version has come to us with misprints and mistakes in transcription that distort it to the point of making it almost incomprehensible. My efforts to restore it to its original form have not always been successful, but it has been possible to translate important fragments of it, so that the general meaning of the song is clear."

Here are certain parts of it:

–The god with the terrible face coupled with Roundness and produced the little berries called *poporos*.

–Himahima Marao coupled with the lichen that grows on rocks and produced lichen.

–Height coupled with Altitude and produced the high grasses of the country.

–Cutting Edge coupled with Adze and produced obsidian.

–Climber coupled with Face With a Penetrating Tongue and produced the *ronas* (climbing plants).

But an unfortunate incident occurred. When Ure Vaeiko began reading the tablet he recited the legends at a rapid rate because Thomson had given him liquor to overcome his reluctance, and he did not notice that the tablet he had first been reading had been stealthily replaced with another.

"He was suddenly accused of fraud. Disconcerted, he launched into explanations that Thomson apparently did not understand very well.

"There is something deeply moving in such misunderstandings which arise from the clash of two mentalities operating on different planes. It would be absurd to believe, like certain investigators, that the natives systematically tried to disappoint them. They were not ignorant people, as is shown by the scanty information we have on them. Responsibility for those lost opportunities falls entirely on the Europeans."

And so the problem is posed. I will reproduce the top line of a page of the Tomenika manuscript, with Latin letters above the ideograms, as they appear in the original text (see the photographic section of this book);

On the right is "To ma ni ka Ava." We know that this is the Tomenika manuscript. But on the left is "Ure Vae iku," which is obviously Ure Vaeiko. So the "impostor" was none other than the man who dictated this precious document to Tomenika, so that the tradition would not be lost. What, then, are we to think of Thomson in this affair?

In the light of what Ure Vaeiko said, let us try to see if several signs from two other lines may not be related to the genealogical lists that were known to him. It would be surprising if he had not dictated them to Tomenika. But we will not go very far in that direction because, as Métraux says, Thomson's version is incomplete and distorted.

4. Cutting Edge

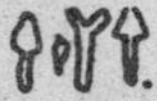

. . coupled with Adze

. and produced obsidian.

In another part of the manuscript the signs . . appear. I believe they represent a vase or other recipient made of stone, perhaps obsidian.

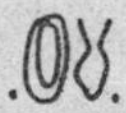

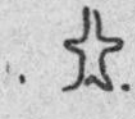

. . Height

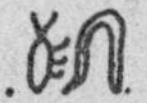

. . coupled with Altitude

. and produced the high grasses of the country.

. . The god with the terrible face (perhaps the god whose face was dangerous to look upon?)

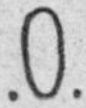

. . coupled with Roundness

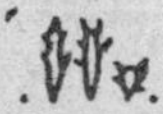

. . and produced the little *poporo* berries.

. Climber (whom we have already seen above, associated with Altitude)

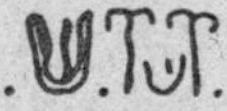

. . . coupled with Face With a Penetrating Tongue

. and produced the *ronas* (climbing plants).

. . Himahima Marao (?) (The syllable "ma" occurs three times.)

coupled with the lichen that grows on rocks

and produced lichen.

This sign designates "the lichen that grows on rocks." But its oblique line suggests the spoor of moss at the time when its opening releases its contents , lichen.

In Chapter 4 we saw a similar sign for the opening of the egg and its contents, the embryo , which becomes the chick of the sea swallow, *manu taru*.

To return to lichen , it is represented here by several different signs. Métraux reports that the ancient Easter Islanders were enthusiastic botanists and distinguished several varieties within a single plant species, sometimes by minute details.

Punctuation plays a major part in the composition and understanding of *rongo-rongo* writing. But you may have noticed an anomaly in the preceding line. In translating, for example, "Height coupled with Altitude and produced the high grasses of the country," we see that the scribe placed the dots as follows:

We should therefore read, "The high grasses of the

country were produced by Height, after Height had coupled with Altitude."

The same is also true of the following two sentences. "Cutting Edge coupled with Adze and produced obsidian."

"Climber coupled with Face With a Penetrating Tongue and produced the *ronas*."

The persistence of this shift in punctuation, in relation to ideas concerning genealogy, strengthens my conviction that these successive sentences refer to Ure Vaeiko's narrative.

But I will stop here because the difficulty of the task is obvious, particularly in identifying Himahima Marao, Face With a Penetrating Tongue, Climber, and so on. It would take sources of more precise information. Are they forever lost? If so, there are lines of *rongo-rongo* writing that can never be translated fully.

If, as has been said, Tomenika was one of Katherine Routledge's informers, he dtd not tell her very much. Not about essential matters, at least.

Relations between Thomson and Ure Vaeiko were quickly and irremediably broken off.

But let us not lose sight of the fact that after the discovery of Easter Island by Europeans, nearly all their contacts with the people of the island were marked by tragedies, up to the atrocity of 1862. In view of that, it is surprising that the last survivors who knew the secrets of the island were reluctant to reveal them, especially the secret of a writing which, by a kind of extreme restraint, "speaks without asserting"?

As for the transportation of the statues, it clearly shows the difference of mentality, the two planes mentioned by Alfred Métraux:

—The Easter Islanders have deliberately kept only the idea of *mana*.

—The Europeans have sought only the material, practical explanation.

Even if it turns out that this latter explanation is now known, I cannot say too often that only *mana* mattered, because otherwise we would be seeing Easter Island in the light of our own ideas, and not as it really was. That is why I wrote at the beginning of this book, "*Mana* . . . was a necessity. It was necessity itself. Without it, nothing would have had any meaning on Easter Island."

Let us forget the ropes . . .

CHAPTER EIGHT

Rongo-Rongo Writing and Chinese Writing

The question of parallels between the *rongo-rongo* writing of Easter Island and other writings has often been raised.

The linguist Guillaume de Hevesy found similarities between Easter Island symbols and those of a five-thousand-year-old writing in the towns of Mohenjo-Daro and Harappa, in the Indus Valley. Alfred Métraux maintains that the relation between the two writings is not as close as Hevesy believed.

Dr. Heine Geldern pointed out strong resemblances between *rongo-rongo* signs and certain archaic Chinese characters, particularly from the Shang period.

We will use a few examples to judge these links between archaic Chinese writing and that of Easter Island. There are certain resemblances not only in the forms of the characters, but also in their meanings. I will use only Easter Island signs that I have interpreted in a sustained context, and not in isolation. I will classify the comparisons under three headings:

a) Resemblance of form, different meanings.
b) Resemblance of form, same meaning.
c) Complete analogy.

For the sake of convenience I will designate Easter Island writing simply as "Easter," and archaic Chinese writing as "China."

The ancient Chinese signs and their interpretations are taken from *L'Écriture chinoise et le geste humain,* by B. Tchang Tcheng Ming (Paris, Librairie Geuthner), and *Chinese Characters,* by Leon Wieger (Formosa, Kuangchi Press).

a) *Resemblance of form, different meanings.*

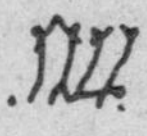

1 Easter: two men pulling a rope (Chapter 6).

China: two men fighting.

Easter: horizontal man: man swimming (Chapter 4).

China: horizontal man: adversity, but also the idea of going against something.

Easter: going forward in semicircles, first in one direction, then in the other (Chapter 6).

China: looking in both directions.

b) *Resemblance of form, same meaning.*

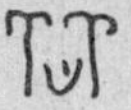

Easter: face (Chapter 7).

China: face.

Easter: heart (Chapter 3).

China: heart.

Easter: sea (Chapters 4 and 6).

China: water.

Easter: demon (Chapter 5).

China: demon. (Note the similarity between the two forked heads.)

Easter: stone cave in a cliff (Chapter 4).

China: cliff.

China: stone, rock.

Easter: moon (Chapter 3).

China: moon.

Easter: sea swallow (Chapter 4).

China: swallow.

c) *Complete analogy.*

Easter: height (Chapter 7).

China: man standing, seen from the front: tall.

Easter: lifting the hat onto the statue (Chapter 1).

Easter: successive positions of the hat, represented by the four circles.

Easter: upward movement.

China: rise, slope.

Easter: the idea of sound, in the term "listening to the bird" (Chapter 4).

China: hand + drum + sticks = sound of a drum.

We thus see that in Easter Island writing the idea of sound is expressed in the same way: by the beating of sticks on a drum. It is known that the Easter Islanders had stone drums.

o Easter: In Easter Island writing a circle conveys the idea of Knowledge and the mystical force of *mana.* When placed on the symbol of a person, it indicates that he is an initiate or a king.

China: prince, master.

The circle represents a flame above a lamp. The prince or master "rises" above others like a flame, and is seen by everyone.

The circle also has the meaning of "the eye of doctrine."

After seeing the thought-provoking resemblances between the two writings, we cannot help raising certain questions. Was an Asian civilization brought to Easter Island? If so, it must first have been brought to eastern Polynesia, starting point of the migration led by Hotu Matua, since legends say explicitly that it was he who brought writing, first inscribed on banana leaves, then later carved in *toro miro* wood to make it last longer, so that tradition could be preserved.

Persuasive though this argument may seem, however, it is not decisive, since statues from the first period, before Hotu Matua's arrival, bear carved signs that strongly resemble certain ancient Chinese characters.

Or did ancient peoples, very close to nature and "immediate" knowledge of it, use similar signs to give simple expression to what they saw in a simple way? Does this explain the resemblances between the two ancient writings?

But here is the most disturbing question: Why do Easter Island statues from the first period have hands so strangely similar to those of Asian statues, with thumbs curved upward and long, tapering fingernails? On their backs they have this inscription, to which I will return in a later chapter:

Aside from similarities in writing, let us recall the Easter Island sign for the master sculptor who makes the first outline of a statue on the stone from which it will be carved. He holds a square, and the first meaning is that he makes regularly spaced holes in the stone to mark off the future statue.

The deep meaning of this sign is found in Chinese thought. The square is a yang symbol: the symbol of action, work and builders. To be complete, we must say that it is also the symbol of land, and therefore a yin symbol, because plots of land are marked off with right angles. And the Whole can be constituted only when there is coexistence and interpenetration of yang and yin.

This point—the correlation between the signification of the Chinese sign and the deep, even metaphysical meaning of the corresponding Easter Island sign—is so important that it will be the subject of the last chapter of this book.

CHAPTER NINE

Transmission of *Rongo-Rongo* Writing

It is now time to discuss the Tomenika manuscript in greater detail. Tomenika was one of Katherine Routledge's informants.* She stayed on Easter Island in 1914. Her work on the subject is still authoritative.

As it exists now, the manuscript contains forty-one pages covered with ideograms. It was shown to Thor Heyerdahl in 1956, then given to Francis Mazière when he left the island in 1964.

It is written in an account book from the Chilean navy. Its last Easter Island owner said that he had received it from his father, who had in turn received it from his grandfather. When one copy was worn out, a new one was made. Judging from the photograph of it that Mazière published in *Mysteries of Easter Island,* the last copy, known as the Tomenika manuscript, is in extremely dilapidated condition.

It is a unique document, recording almost the

*He died soon after her arrival.

whole of Easter Island writing for posterity. Yet some names and sentences in it are written in Latin characters. The explanation is that some of the survivors who returned from Peru after the deportation of 1862 had learned to write with Latin characters. In Chapter 7 we saw a line of ideograms surmounted by the names of Tomenika and Ure Vaeiko:

Ure vae.iku To ma nika ava

In interpreting this line, we must bear in mind that carved wood was called *kohua rongo-rongo,* which means literally "transmitters of writing." By extension, this idea also applies to the writing on paper that concerns us here. By the names surmounting it, the line above illustrates the way in which this writing was transmitted, resulting in the famous manuscript.

We must first note the gestures of the figures that show how the precious message is received and then transmitted. To make this clearer, I will omit several intermediate signs and, for the time being, consider only these five:

Ure vae.iku To ma nika ava

The personages are sometimes drawn as Long-Ears and sometimes in the guise of the birdman, who is an embodiment of divine power and therefore an initiate.

A man (birdman) has the message and makes the gesture of transmitting it.

The three following signs are the same representation of Ure Vaeiko, under whose name they are placed:

Ure vae iku

Ure Vaeiko (Long-Ear) receives the message.

Ure Vaeiko (birdman) will retranscribe it on wood.

Ure Vaeiko, again a Long-Ear, gives the writing to his "successor." His arm is depicted as a branch, probably of the *toro miro* tree, to illustrate the fact that the writing was initially carved in wood.

To ma ni ka ava

Finally Tomenika receives the written word from Ure Vaeiko. The broad gesture of his left arm designates his name, and also the contents of the message he will convey, as we will see.

Having established this, we can now begin reading the whole line, from left to right.

A man, in the guise of the birdman, has received knowledge of *rongo-rongo* writing. He transmits the message to Ure Vaeiko, who takes a branch of the *toro miro* tree and squares it to give it the form of a two-faced tablet (the little branches are there to show again that it is a two-faced wooden tablet).

Here is the tablet in its final form: . (We will recall this representation of carved wood in Chapter 4: .)

. On this tablet Ure Vaeiko inscribes the message and gives it to the man who will next take possession of it. Two tablets are shown here, simply to indicate that both faces were covered with signs, and also, since there is a repetition of the character, that Ure Vaeiko carved several tablets.

Tomenika receives the writing and retranscribes it. What does he write? We see these ideograms under his name: .

As we could expect, we see here the emblem of each of the main subjects we have examined through this writing:

The birdman cult (Chapter 4).

The demon, as he was in Chapter 5, dealing with the origin of the *moai kava-kava* statuary.

The transportation of the statues, and the men who made them (Chapters 1 and 2).

The birth of a child (Chapter 3). A birdman here holds an umbilical cord, for understanding of this phenomenon was not, of course, limited to initiates, even though it had a divine essence.

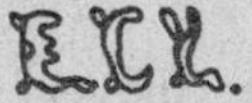

[rongorongo signs]. Finally these umbilical cords, of varying shapes, which correspond to the various origins of life in this world, as is related in the genealogical songs (Chapter 7).

[rongorongo sign] The origin of the divinities and of women. I attribute a feminine meaning to this sign because its lower part is prolonged; other ideograms representing a woman, or women in general, have the same aspect:

[rongorongo sign] The woman who gives the sculptor the crown of ferns (Chapter 2).

At this point I will make a digression on the sign [rongorongo sign], the corpse of Ku'uku'u (Chapter 1). The lower part seems to be prolonged, but that can be explained by the fact that there is asymmetry between the left side of the body and the right side, the one turned toward Hiva, which seems larger, and this has the effect of lengthening the arm and the leg.

The left side is tapered, like the symbol of death beside it [rongorongo sign], in which life seems to be fleeing.

In any case, all this is found in the sign [rongorongo sign], "His current of life, starting from Hiva, grows and then dies out on Easter Island."

Statue from the first period.
(Rano Raraku volcano.)
PHOTOGRAPH F. MAZIÈRE.

Ure vae iku Te ma mka ava

FIRMA

Fecha

Pages from the notebook of RONGO-RONGO *writing used for Dr. Schwartz's translations. This unique notebook was given to Tila Mazière by Veriveri, the last initiate of the Island of Silence.* PHOTOGRAPHY F. MAZIÈRE.

The seven sacred statues (second period) which look toward the northwest, toward the Land of Hiva. PHOTOGRAPH F. MAZIÈRE.

A statue unearthed by the French expedition to Easter Island. In it, hands with long fingernails appeared for the first time. PHOTOGRAPH F. MAZIÈRE.

Birdman. Statuette of TORO MIRO *wood, five and a half inches high.* MAZIÈRE PRIVATE COLLECTION.

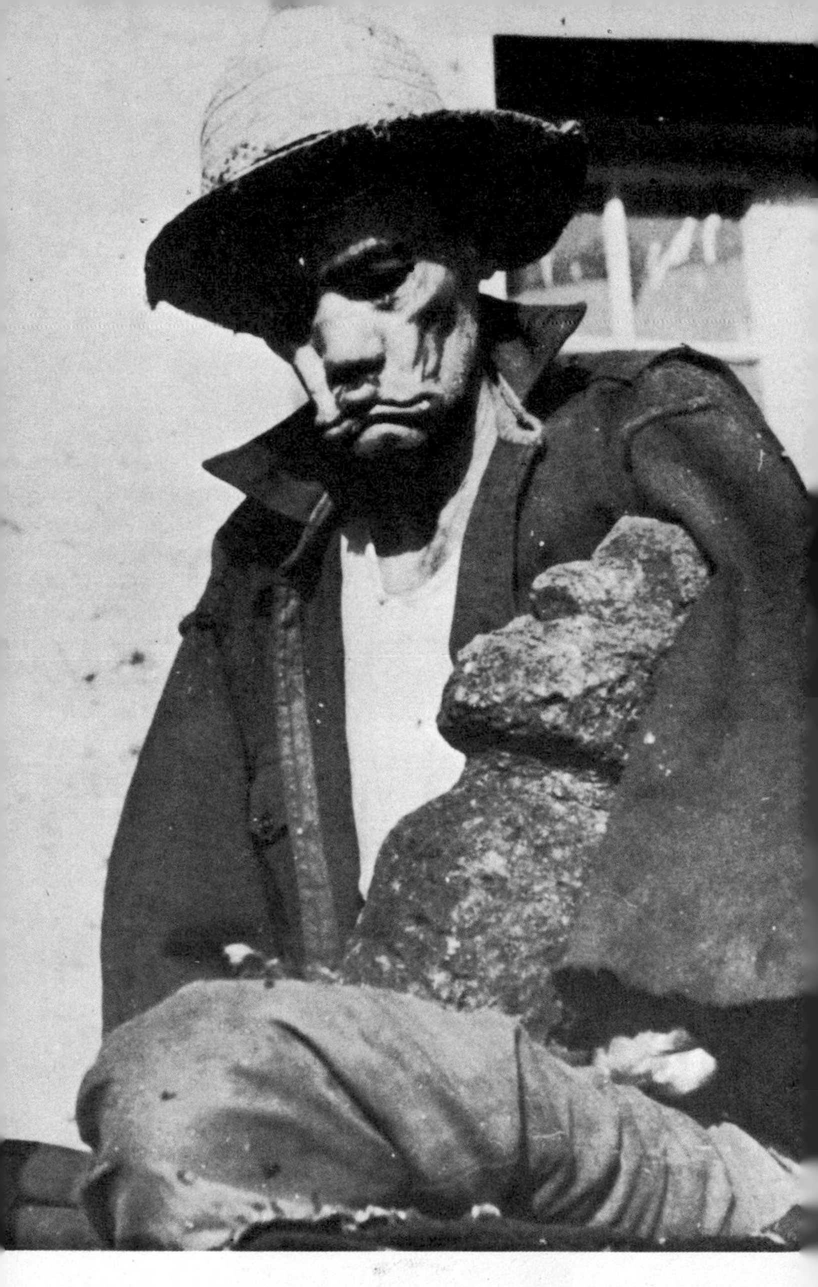

Gabriel Veriveri, the last initiate of the Island of Silence. He died of leprosy. PHOTOGRAPH F. MAZIÈRE.

This sign  therefore has nothing in common with a sign prolonged at the bottom, representing a woman, like those we are now considering, and particularly the following, the woman ancestor:

The woman ancestor (Chapter 13).

In the Tomenika manuscript the origin of mankind now appears.

. And finally the origin of animals, and perhaps also of plants.

At the end of this line we can note the apparently strange fact that many of the ideograms seem to have ears:

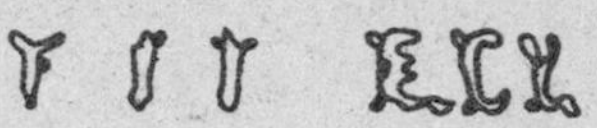

Tomenika and his predecessors apparently wanted to stress the point that everything had its explanation and origin in the knowledge of the noble, dominant class, the Long-Ears. They therefore put ears on many signs, from umbilical cords to wooden tablets, from statues to the stone winch that we will see in the next line. But then, having thoroughly established the point, they seem to have felt that there was no longer any need to keep stressing it so often. The lines we have previously studied (which, in the manuscript, are below this one) contain fewer signs marked with ears, as if the scribe considered it useless to go on repeating that distinctive emblem.

CHAPTER TEN

Dorsal Inscriptions and Lifting the Hats

We began our study of *rongo-rongo* writing in the chapter devoted to the transportation of the statues. But once a statue had been taken to its final destination and installed on its *ahu,* it still had to receive its hat of red volcanic stone in order to be complete. I described the principle of lifting the hat in Chapter 1; we will now see how it is illustrated in another line of ideograms.

This line is composed of three parts.

–One part depicts the lifting of the hat.

–Another explains and defines the knowledge of the Long-Ears.

—Another clearly shows that the Easter Islanders attributed life to their statues.

A general meaning emerges from the three-part division of this line. We will return to it later, but for the moment it can be summarized as follows. Those stone giants had life and *mana*. All traditions of the island agree in saying that it was the head that bore *mana*. I conclude that the stone hat was the seat of that mystical force. Life and *mana* were communicated to the statues by the high knowledge of that fantastic race, the Long-Ears.

We will read the line in its entirety, going from left to right.

First part

The association of four signs not separated by punctuation gives the meaning of movement. In this case it is the movement of life possessed by the statues. It is evoked by the flow of blood from the heart.

The heart, with the arch and trunk of the aorta, at which the intercostal arteries begin. It is amazing to note that this representation is the same as those in our anatomy textbooks.

The statue seen from the front (see Chapter

6: statue seen from the front* ( ).

These two signs will be fused with each other. To illustrate this fusion better, the scribe draws them both in profile.

The heart, seen in profile.

Still in profile, the fusion of the heart and the statue. We now see the association, in the minds of the Easter Island initiates, of blood flowing in the stone statue and giving it life.

This is related to the Easter Island legend that the dead had prominent veins. These statues were consecrated to worship of the dead and therefore had to have their own circulatory system, as Tomenika shows us.

Second part

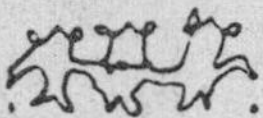

. . Three Long-Ears.

The Long-Ears were slaughtered by the Short-Ears (see Chapter 1). Certain legends say that when the Long-Ears were killed in the ditch on the Poike peninsula, three of them managed to escape. This ideogram might be regarded as a reference to that event, but it seems to contain a deeper meaning: "Three is the symbol of Knowledge."

We know that in Easter Island writing three associ-

*It is in the context of the writing that I say "from the front," as distinct from "in profile," but it should be remembered that the circle was inscribed on the back of the statue.

ated elements designate an object, and therefore knowledge of that object:

Carved wood (Chapter 4).

Statue (Chapter 6).

Priest's stick (Chapter 5).

Statues from the first period have three signs inscribed on their backs:

These three signs represent three elements of the universe, which we will discuss later. But does not knowledge consist of union with the universe?

. . I will say, then, that the sign represents three Long-Ears possessing Knowledge: three initiates or "learned men."

. That is why these three signs, not separated by punctuation, illustrate the domain of the Long-Ears' Knowledge.

The Long-Ears knew demons (see Chapter 5) and the spirits called *aku-*

akus, which played such an important part in the life and legends of the island.

They also knew the deep nature of man.

This calls for explanation. We have seen other signs surmounted by a small line:

. . Tuu Ko Ihu cut down a tree with a stone axe (see Chapter 5).

. . The statue moves forward in semicircles, on its convex base (see Chapter 6). The small line thus indicates either a movement of rotation in the horizontal plane or a movement of oscillation in the vertical plane.

Here we have the sign . I believe it represents a dance, with a movement of oscillation from one foot to the other.

Tila Mazière has told me that such dances are performed in Polynesia. Their purpose is to engender an inner state in which man experiences, through that movement, spiritual union with the universe around him. The "liberation" that leads to this union is similar in its meaning to the practice of yoga, except that in yoga it is obtained through immobility.

Manifested by the movement of the dance , it is this union of man with the world that I here call Knowledge.

. Finally, the statues and the writing belonged to

the Long-Ears, which is why there is a mixture of two representations in this sign:

A statue (see Chapter 6: a statue seen from the front).

A wooden tablet with *rongo-rongo* writing on it (Chapter 9).

And because this sign is a fusion of the two above, Tomenika drew four ears on it.

THIRD PART

The lifting of the hat of Knowledge onto the statue. Let us briefly recall the technique employed (Chapter 1). On a ramp of ropes passing over the flat head of the statue, the hat was lifted by a stone winch to which it was attached. The winch was moved by other ropes which also passed over the statue.

. . Three categories of men were needed for this enterprise: the Short-Ears (shown without ears) who held the ropes that formed the supporting ramp; the Short-Ears who pulled the ropes that made the winch and the hat rise; and of course the Long-Ears, who invented this method of lifting the hat onto the statue.

. . This is an extraordinary ideogram:

The lifting of the hat.

The ramp of ropes.

This symbol shows the upward movement of the hat, with an indication of the ropes attaching it to the winch:

. Here is the stone winch. It is shown with ears. Tomenika would not have forgotten to include them in the representation of such an important part of the system used in erecting the statues.

. Ropes passing over the head of the statue.

The statue, still with ears, is represented by a sign divided into three parts; as we have seen, this designates an object.

It rests on a flared base: its *ahu*.

It is surmounted by a small dot. This is one of the few cases in Easter Island writing (and it is very discreet) where we find an evocation of a statue with its hat in place. There is a reason for this, which we will discuss at the end of this book: there was no need for the hat to appear in writing.

At the end of the line is proof that the hat was not lifted until the statue was on its *ahu*, that it was lifted by means of a winch, and that both were supported during their upward motion by ropes passing over the statue.

. ·The line ends with this Long-Ear, whom Tomenika shows in a triumphant "pose" beside the ropes that were used in moving the statues and lifting the hats, because their concept and application were the fruit of the Long-Ears' imagination and genius.

In his arm  we find this part  of the ideogram  . designating the double system of ropes used in transporting the statues. The same is true of the representation of the birdman in Chapter 2:  .

Three basic ideas are thus expressed by the line:

—The Easter Islanders believed that the statues had life.

—Knowledge belonged to the Long-Ears.

—That Knowledge was transmitted to the statue by its hat, as is shown by the fact that the line ends with the lifting of the hat.

Another fact supports the assertion that the hat is a symbol of Knowledge: *it is red.*

Before going any further, let us return to this

image of the statue bearing its hat in which the hat is indicated simply by a dot. (In the Tomenika manuscript the ideograms are drawn in black, but this dot is red.)

In China, cinnabar, or *red* mercuric sulfide, the emblem and symbol of alchemy and all its implied knowledge of matter through a special vision and philosophical research, was indicated by a dot in a melting pot: .

When the first European travelers came to Easter Island in the eighteenth century, the statues did not have the same appearance they have now: several of them were painted. Traces of that paint have been found on the bases of a few statues still inserted in their *ahus*. So there was nothing to prevent the Easter Islanders from making the hats in the same quarry where they made the statues, on the Rano Raraku volcano, and then painting them red, a color they had at their disposal. Or they could have made each statue in a single piece, including the hat. But they did neither. A deep reason made them perform the immense labor of taking the hats from another volcano, Puna Pau, and transporting them separately to the statues: *the stone of Puna Pau is red in its natural state.*

Legends will help us to understand this necessity better.

When Tuu Ko Ihu had the idea of carving a piece of *toro miro* wood and thus giving birth to the little *moai kava-kava* statuary, he had seen a demon leaning against a section of *red* stone. This detail, included in a legend concerning a fundamental subject, has been preserved through the ages, probably because it contains an important meaning.

In Chapter 5 we saw the demon leaning against that stone: .

Gabriel Veriveri, the last initiate of Easter Island, told Francis Mazière that the statues facing southward "transmit their power to an enormous red volcanic stone which limits the triangle of the Pacific islands."

Another fact is of interest here: the oldest statues, dating from before Hotu Matua's arrival and the statues known as those of the first period, *are made of red stone*. First there is the famous triangular head of an old man, and then there is the headless column, with a sketchy indication of arms crossed over the belly, discovered by Heyerdahl; it is strangely reminiscent of certain sculptured columns at Tiahuanaco and in another part of South America that we will have occasion to discuss later.

Thus the hats had to be made of red stone, perhaps in order to communicate with the magic red stone mentioned by Gabriel Veriveri, and also to maintain contact with the "great ancestors" immortalized in red stone.

One question immediately arises: How did the Easter Islanders, who placed that emblem of Knowledge on their statues, know the importance of choosing that color, when they belonged to a Polynesian migration later than the twelfth century, whereas the red statues date from a much earlier time? Only one answer seems plausible to me: when they reached the island they found not only the oldest statues and those from the first period, but also survivors of the preceding civilization who told them, among other things, that the southward-facing statues looked toward the red volcanic stone which kept their power and Knowledge. Then, having found the Puna Pau quarry, with its red stone answering to their need for that color, they used it for the hats of their statues.

The fact that the successive civilizations of Easter Island have all been in contact with each other, if only at times when one of them arrived and the preceding one was about to disappear, seems to be of fundamental importance in understanding that "end of the earth."

It is involved, for example, in the fact that the statues of the second period, erected by Hotu Matua's people and their descendants, all have their backs to the sea: they face away from the original homeland, Hiva. It is not known if that homeland was in the Marquesas or Gambier Islands, or if it was two islands called Marae Renga by legend, part of a vanished archipelago named Hiva.

When Hotu Matua and his people landed on Easter Island, the last survivors of the first period told them that all their statues at the foot of the southwestern side of Rano Raraku were facing away from their original homeland. They stand with their backs to South America and the lands east of it. They therefore face westward, and it is easy to understand why legends say that they are looking for Hiva.

It may seem, however, that this is only a coincidence, later interpreted by the Polynesian newcomers. The fact that the statues of the first period face away from South America may not have been intentional. The stone for them was taken from the outer wall of the crater on the southwest side because that was the part of the volcano best suited to the operation, and they were then erected at the foot of the volcano on that same side, with the result that they stand with their backs to the east, the direction from which their sculptors are said to have come.

When Hotu Matua's Polynesians found that almost the whole outer wall of the crater on the southwest side had already been quarried, they went to work on the inner wall. Not only did they copy the statues of the first period, but *they also adopted the meaning of their orientation: they too erected their statues facing away from their original land, Hiva.*

But as we will see at the end of this book, besides this hypothesis there is one based on quite different and much deeper arguments that will appear only after a long inquiry.

A strange impression arises from all this: all the statues of Easter Island, those giants from both periods, with disdainful lips, look at each other and turn their backs on their sculptors' homeland. It is as if the orientation of those "prisoners for life on that strip of land where life is dying" (Mazière) implied a final renunciation of the impossible idea of escape.

Yet there are some exceptions to that rule.

–Seven statues of the second period look toward Hiva. But there is the legend of the first seven explorers of the Polynesian migration: six sons of kings went off to make preparations for Hotu Matua's arrival, and with them went the spirit of Hau Maka, who had announced that voyage to Matakiterani;

there were thus seven of them. It may be that, to honor their memory, one of the few exceptions was made by placing those seven statues so that they faced the sea.

—We have seen, in *rongo-rongo* writing, that the Orongo statue faced the sea: . That famous statue is now called the "Wave Breaker," but the Easter Islanders called it the "Statue With the Power to Balance Things." To keep its strange power it had to face the sea toward which it exercised that power.

—Finally there were the mysterious statues on an *ahu* cut into the face of the Orongo cliff; in the "statue-overthrowing time" they were toppled into the sea.

DORSAL INSCRIPTIONS ON THE STATUES

Statues of the first period have these three signs inscribed on their backs:

Certain *ahus* date from that period. One of them is the Ahu Vinapu, whose architecture, with its convex, beveled stone slabs, is related to the pre-Incan style.

Radioactive carbon datings place its construction in the eighth century A.D.

But although the arrangements of stones in that *ahu* recalls certain structures in South America—in Peru, for example—it is still true that the signs on the backs of the statues are similar in form and meaning to certain archaic Chinese signs. They are symbols of the elements of the universe: sun, sea, earth, with an extension concerning the circle.

In ancient Chinese writing:

⊙ The circle, bcsides its meaning of sunlight, also has that of Knowledge, the "eye of doctrine."

Water.

A mountain. And for a volcanic island like Easter Island, it would be hard to imagine a better representation of the earth than this sign:

But, along with these inscriptions, let us remember that the statues of the first period have hands with long, tapering fingernails and upturned thumbs. The dorsal signs and the long fingernails are the mark of a civilization that came from much farther away than South America, or from a totally different direction. We will have to give further attention to this problem of the direction from which civilization was brought to Easter Island, because it is of fundamental importance.

An Easter Islander said to Francis Mazière, "The first race invented *rongo-rongo* writing and inscribed it in stone. The only other place where that writing still exists is in Asia."

CHAPTER ELEVEN

The Long-Ears
Creation of the World
The Magic Word

THE LONG-EARS

The first Polynesian migration, led by King Hotu Matua, reached Easter Island in about the twelfth century. Five generations later, in the thirteenth century, the second Polynesian migration was led by King Anua Motua, who made an extraordinary voyage that took him close to Tierra del Fuego before bringing him to Easter Island. Legends say that it was he who brought the race known as the Long-Ears, Hanau Eepe.

Hotu Matua's people were Short-Ears, Hanau Momoko. There is every reason to believe that they were subjugated by the Long-Ears who arrived in the second migration.

Father Sebastian Englert, the priest who lived forty years on Easter Island, recently made an assertion based on a question of pronunciation: according to him, "Hanau Eepe" does not mean "Long-Ears," but "Fat Men." Despite his meticulousness (it was he who painted a large number on each statue), he may have lost sight of the fact that all the statues on the island have long ears and do not suggest fatness.

Then the Short-Ears rebelled against their masters, the Long-Ears, and slaughtered them, as I have said earlier.

Several reasons prompt me to state a personal opinion concerning the Long-Ears, reasons that are situated almost at the two extremes of Easter Island history.

First, all statues of the first period, dating from before the arrival of Anua Motua and the people known as the Long-Ears, have long ears.

When the first European travelers discovered Easter Island in the eighteenth century, they reported that the natives had ears whose lobes hung down to their shoulders. Their lobes were stretched by piercing them and hanging heavy pieces of shark backbone from them.

Finally, there is the statement made to Francis Mazière by an Easter Islander: "The first inhabitants of the island were survivors of the world's first race. They were yellow and very tall, with long arms, huge chests, *big ears, but without stretched lobes.* Pure blond hair and hairless, shiny bodies. They did not have fire. Long ago, that race lived on two Polynesian islands. They came in boats from a land behind America."

I have attached great importance to Easter Island legends. The people to whom oral traditions were transmitted kept them intact, especially in an isolated world like Easter Island. Yet we must be willing to accept a legitimate phenomenon of distortion in these stories, beyond the curve of the horizon of time or space. The last sentence, "They came in boats from a land beyond America," is especially perplexing and I will analyze it in the chapter dealing with the origin of the Easter Islanders. Nevertheless, this legend seems fundamental to me.

We are thus faced with the problem of civilization brought to the island before the arrival of Hotu Matua's Polynesians in the twelfth century. Several hypotheses can be considered.

The statues of the earliest period (fourth century?), including the red head of an old man and especially the sculptured red column, which recalls similar works found in South America, may be evidence of a first influence that came from the east.

And according to Mazière's informant the real Long-Ears also came from the east. Those people, skilled sculptors who had mastered the techniques of a gigantic statuary like that found in Peru, erected large statues whose bases were buried in the ground at the foot of Rano Raraku and built *ahus* in pre-Incan style, including the Ahu Vinapu, which datings by radioactive carbon situate in the eighth century.

But at this point a difficulty arises. Their statues, known as those of the first period, have tapering fingernails and dorsal signs identical with certain signs in ancient Chinese writing. Must we therefore assume that, between the two migrations we have discussed, there was an "Asian" migration which came from the west and left no trace but those two features of the statues?

At this stage in our study, however, those two features do not enable us to reach a conclusion on the exact origin of that civilization. Other arguments can be put forward. There are disturbing similarities between archaic Chinese writing and the Easter Island ideograms, but we must remember that other similarities between ancient writings can be pointed out. For example, the Easter Island signs have been compared with those of Mohenjo-Daro, in the Indus Valley, and with ancient Egyptian hieroglyphics. Resemblances actually exist between writings from widely separated regions.

As we will see later, there seems to be a missing element in the sequence of historical events on the island, expecially with regard to the "Asian" influence between the first period and the one before it. Paradoxically, that missing element is earlier than Hotu Matua's arrival, yet is closely related to it: it can only be Marae Renga, two islands of the Hiva Archipelago. I am forced to believe that they disappeared as the result of a cataclysm, as legend says. They formed the necessary link between Asia and Easter Island. That link will be discussed in the last chapter of this book.

Except for a few survivors, those three civilizations vanished: the oldest one, the "Asian" intermediary, and that of the first period.

Twelfth century: arrival of Hotu Matua and the Short-Ears, who originated in Polynesia, west of Easter Island. They brought *rongo-rongo* writing with them. Since the influence of southern China was strong in Polynesia, and perhaps even more so in Marae Renga, we shoud not be too surprised by the similarities between *rongo-rongo* signs and archaic Chinese writing: the common origin is west of Easter Island.

Thirteenth century: the voyage of Anua Motua and his people, who were called the Long-Ears. *This is where the confusion arises.* They subjugated the Short-Ears, and perhaps "Hanua Eepe" really does mean "Fat Men." But the essential point is that when they took power over the island and saw stone idols with long ears, they *artificially lengthened* their ears. Not only did they copy the statues they found on the island, creating those known as the statues of the second period, but after they had taken power they decided to make themselves resemble those stone "gods" by taking on their most distinctive feature: long ears.

Then the Short-Ears exterminated that people with artificially lengthened ears. When the Short-Ears had taken control of the island they also lengthened their earlobes until they hung down to their shoulders, as was described by the Europeans who saw them in the eighteenth century. But according to legend the first race, the real Long-Ears, had large ears *without stretched lobes.* They came to the island before the eighth century. The statues of the first period are in the image of that legendary race. Is it not surprising to think that each of the successive migrations to Easter Island, coming from the east and then from the west, left a few survivors who transmitted the precious heritage to their successors who had come from a different direction? Perhaps that explains the ancient name of Easter Island: Te Pito no te Henua, "Navel of the World."

The island seems to have a special destiny. After the most recent Polynesian population had come from the west, a civilization from the east was brought first by Europeans, then by Chileans.

Be that as it may, since *rongo-rongo* writing is the main basis of this book we will examine it to see the importance of that question related to the length of ears. Their size establishes a hierarchy in representations of individuals. The longer the ears, the greater the degree of nobility or initiation, regardless of whether the circle of *mana* is present or not.

Sculptor (Chapter 2).

Master sculptor (Chapter 2).

Priest in charge of transporting statues (Chapter 2).

Priest whose function is to tie the umbilical cord (Chapter 3).

The god Make-Make (Chapter 11).

There are also signs for objects which are shown with ears to stress their relation to the Long-Ears.

Statue (Chapter 6).

Carved tablet (Chapter 9).

Umbilical cord (Chapter 9).

Stone winch (Chapter 10).

Heart (Chapter 10).

When we discuss the origin of the Easter Islanders, we will have occasion to speak of a "common center in Asia" as the departure point of Easter Island civilization in ancient times. In India and China, the length of ears is an extremely important point. Some statues of Buddha have ears with inordinately long lobes, like the head of Buddha, dating from the beginning of the Christian era, in the Sarnath museum. "In China, the most notable symbolism is that of long ears, a sign of wisdom and immortality. Lao-tse had ears seven inches long; he was sometimes known as Long-Ears. This was also true of several other illustrious and exceptionally long-lived men, such as Wukuang, Yuan-k'ieu and the prodigious legendary hero of secret societies, Chu Chuen-mei."*

CREATION OF THE WORLD

Francis Mazière has gathered two legends concerning the creation of the world and mankind. Here are some extracts from them:

> The first vibration, the first word
> that created light . . .

**Dictionnaire des Symboles*. *Paris*, Robert Laffont, 1969.

There came the sun, the great light;
There came the moon, the small light;
There came the stars.
Kuihi-Kuaha (a magic word).
There camé Make-Make, the first man . . .
There came a white bird . . .
It cried, "Kuihi-Kuaha."

In the line of the Tomenika manuscript that follows the one we discussed in the chapter on genealogies, there is this series of signs:

. The first word, represented by this ribbon coming from a mouth. In ancient Chinese writing the mouth is written: and speech:

. The sound corresponding to this word (see Chapter 4: symbol of sound.)

. There came a white bird

which uttered a cry (see Chapter 4: the cry.)

, These two signs, not separated by punctuation, can only correspond to the magic word: Kuihi-Kuaha.

. There came the sun, the great light.

There came the moon, the small light (see Chapter 3: the moon.)

. . There came the stars.

. . There came Make-Make, the first man (surrounded by stars.)

Make-Make, the god of Easter Island, is shown here in the guise of the first man, and he has gigantic ears. The writing agrees with legend: the people of the first race had enormous ears.

"The god Make-Make was present everywhere on Easter Island," says Francis Mazière. His face was painted in caves and carved on the rocks of Orongo.

In *rongo-rongo* writing, as an embodiment of the first man, we have seen him represented by this sign:

We find his face in no other place. We may wonder if the "god with the terrible face"  was not, ultimately, Make-Make, the god of birds. Coupling with Roundness  (see Chapter 7), would he not correspond to the perfect form of the egg?

Furthermore we are struck by the resemblance between that "god with the terrible face"  and the demon  in Chapter 3, at least so far as the upper part of the body is concerned. He also resembles this sign in Chapter 3  , which I have here drawn as a silhouette. It represents the cock; that is, a bird.

These two signs  form one of the few pairs, among all those we have seen, which have the same lower part, not to mention the similarity of outline.

.  . Thus in *rongo-rongo* writing the representation of Make-Make is formed by superimposing the bird on the demon. But his presence in that writing is as constant as it was everywhere else. Each time the birdman appears, there is a direct evocation of Make-Make's intervention:

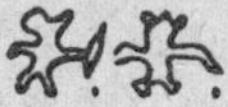

. . . The sculptor receives his stone axe from the birdman (Chapter 2).

. . . The birdman transmits to the initiated

priest the inspiration for the system of transporting statues by means of ropes (Chapter 2).

The birdman holds an umbilical cord (Chapter 9). "Life depended on Make-Make."

. . . The birdman brings the head of Prince Rokoroko Hetau to King Nga Ara; the prince's destiny had been determined by the god, who was the only one capable of opposing such strong *mana* (Chapter 12).

. Finally, in Chapter 9, Ure Vaeiko receives from the birdman the message that he will retranscribe on wood, for *rongo-rongo* writing was marked by a manifestation of the divinity.

It is surprising to note that a person could accomplish his work only if he became inhabited by the god at a certain time. That is why we have seen a change of appearance in two places, a passage from the form of a Long-Ear to that of the birdman.

Chapter 5: . . Tuu Ko Ihu has seen two demons on the way to his house; the idea of the *moai kava-kava* statuary is born in his mind. To cut down the tree from which he will carve the two demons, he transforms himself into the birdman .

Chapter 9: . Ure Vaeiko, a Long-Ear, receiving the written word, can retranscribe it only if he embodies divine power and becomes the birdman , holding in his hand the tablet on which he will carve the *rongo-rongo* writing.

KUIHI-KUAHA, THE MAGIC WORD

"When he had become old, Hotu Matua divided the island among his children. Each of them became the ancestor of a tribe. After making this division, Hotu Matua went to the Rano Kao volcano, climbed to the top of it and sat on one of the rocks facing westward, toward his homeland of Marae Renga. He invoked four gods who lived in his original homeland: 'Kuihi, Kuaha, Tongau, Opapako,' he said, 'the time has come to make the cock crow.' The cock of Marae Renga crowed, and his crowing was heard across the sea. The hour of Hotu Matua's death had come. He turned to his sons and said, 'Take me back.' They carried him to his house, where he died. His body was buried in an *ahu* of Akahanga."*

There came a white bird. It uttered a cry .

Kuihi-Kuaha  , the names of two gods of the original homeland. The signs that represent them come from speech (which we have seen repeatedly as a ribbon coming from a mouth) and from the spirit, which, as we will see in the last chapter, is indicated by this sign:  .

Kuihi-Kuaha: the word and the spirit of the gods.

*Alfred Métraux, *op. cit.*

CHAPTER TWELVE

Mana

Mana. A mystical force. The supernatural power of certain men: initiated priests, the king. It was by *mana* that the king ruled the forces of nature, animals and plants. In *rongo-rongo* writing, some animals and plants bear the distinctive sign of the *mana* that has been communicated to them: the circle, supreme emblem of light and Knowledge. Make-Make, the god of birds and new life, was omnipresent in the world of Easter Island, but everything depended on *mana.*

Mana could kill. Alfred Métraux recounts the legend of little Prince Rokoroko Hetau, son of King Nga Ara:

"His entrance into the world was accompanied by prodigies, which usually announce the birth of a great leader. Many people were devoured by sharks. Sea animals appeared on the shore and attacked anyone who ventured to go there. Finally white hens, previously unknown, began multiplying.

"These wondrous events were manifestations of Rokoroko Hetau's *mana*.

"In the hope of warding off these catastrophes and saving his people, the reigning king had the child abducted and imprisoned in a cave in the Rano Aroi volcano. This proved to be futile because his subjects, convinced of the sacred nature of the 'little chief with the diadem of white feathers,' refused to bring the symbolic standard of royalty to the legitimate heir (one of his brothers). Nga Ara finally ordered the death of the son whose mystical power had such harmful effects."

Such is the legend, and here is the line of ideograms that describes it:

At the center of the line it is shown that *mana* could kill.

On the right: birth of the royal child.

On the left: the extraordinary manifestations that accompanied his entrance into the world.

On the right

. . The royal child is about to be born. Here is the emblem of his royalty: the ribbon that held the "diadem of feathers."

. . . Birth of the royal child, named Rokoroko Hetau. The moment of birth is shown here by the separation of the child . . from his umbilical cord . We saw in Chapter 3 that the child still in its mother's womb is represented by this sign: .

. He uttered his first cry . . That cry had a divine resonance, therefore the circle is inscribed (see the symbol for sound in Chapter 4).

On the left

. Two circles: the very great power of the royal child's *mana*. It was because of his *mana* that his birth was accompanied by remarkable phenomena:

. Sea animals appeared and killed people on the shore (this sign evokes the shape of a seal.)

. White hens were seen for the first time.

These two signs . . are not separated by punctuation; moreover, they are both marked with a circle, because these animals embodied a manifestation of the gods.

. . There were also fantastic storms, with lightning (which is written in ancient Chinese writing) and thunder like a demonic roar. This sign is formed by the fusion of several cries and several demons, as we saw them united  in Chapter 5.

A curious detail: thunder in ancient Chinese writing  resembles lightning  in Easter Island writing.

At the center

. . The little prince's *mana* was so strong . . . (We already know that the head was the seat of *mana*. Here, the two circles of that "doubly strong" mystical force completely replace the head. They also replace the ears, and that may be why there are two circles: otherwise, perhaps, the ears would have had to be drawn inordinately large.)

ooo

. ooo. . . . that, like an absolute taboo . . . (On Easter Island, taboos were marked by superimposed stones.)

.  . . . . it could kill those who approached it. (See Chapter 1: the representation of a corpse is identical there.)

.  . The king, a Long-Ear, could lift taboos; that was one of his greatest functions; he ordered that the little prince be killed.

King Nga Ara's ears seem relatively small. The scribe drew them this way intentionally. He may have meant to show, comparatively, the size that Rokoroko Hetau's ears would have had if he had drawn them; or there may be another meaning, as we will see.

. . The king's order is carried out. A man, in the guise of the birdman, is here bringing the king the prince's head, which was the seat of his *mana*.

. . Yet a statue was erected to him.

Unlike most signs for a statue, this one does not show the head as flat, for it is the statue of a baby, whose fontanels were not closed.

Chinese writing: a baby with fontanels not yet closed.

. . A piece of tapa was then attached to the tail of a sea bird.

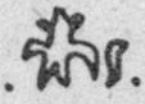

. . And King Nga Ara said, "Go, return to Hiva."

On Easter Island, when a child had been born and the umbilical cord was thrown into the sea, the same words, "Go, return to Hiva," were spoken to signify the return to the origin of the people.

On the little island of Motu Nui, after the discovery of the first egg by the servant of the future birdman, a few sea swallow chicks were kept. When they had grown up, a piece of tapa was attached to one of their legs, they were released and the same words were again spoken: "Return to Hiva."

Tapa is made from bark, which explains the sign attached to the bird  . But there is also another meaning. We have seen the same sign attached to

Ure Vaeiko [rongo-rongo sign] because he transmitted writing on wood.

This bird [rongo-rongo sign] is also the emblem of King Nga Ara because he was one of the greatest scholars of the island. It was he who attached such great importance to schools of *rongo-rongo* writing.

The bird that returns to Hiva carries a branch, which is both a representation of tapa and an indication that King Nga Ara was initiated into writing, like Ure Vaeiko.

When he died, Nga Ara was buried on a litter made of wooden tablets with *rongo-rongo* writing carved on them.

At his court lived a high dignitary whose name has been preserved by tradition: Ure Vaeiko, the same man who was called an impostor.

If we consider all the lines we have interpreted, we see that each of them is oriented around a central group of signs that condition its thought and meaning:

Chapter 1: Transporting the statues [rongo-rongo signs]

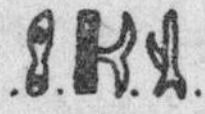

Chapter 2: Making the statues [rongo-rongo signs]

Chapter 3: Birth of a child [rongo-rongo signs]

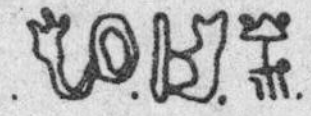

Chapter 4: The birdman cult at Oronga [rongo-rongo signs]

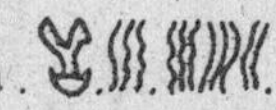

Chapter 5: Origin of the *moai kava-kava* statuary

Chapter 6: Transporting the statues

(Chapter 7, on the genealogical songs, and Chapter 8, on the similarities between *rongo-rongo* writing and ancient Chinese writing, are independent of the others from this point of view.)

Chapter 6: Inspiration of the movement of the statues

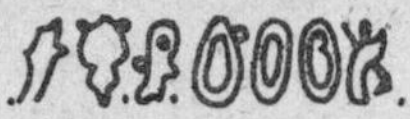

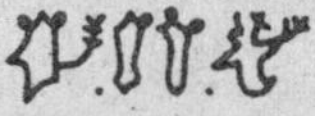

Chapter 9: The transmission of writing

Chapter 10: The Long-Ears' knowledge; lifting the hats of Knowledge

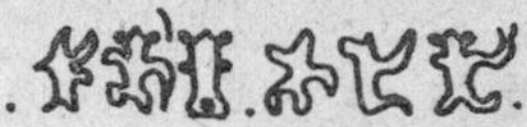

Chapter 11: Creation of the world

Chapter 12: Evocation of the force of *mana*

The persistence of this central theme, which is found in eleven lines, seems to be one of the bases of *rongo-rongo* writing in the Tomenika manuscript. It should also be noted that the end signs of a line play an important part:

Chapter 1: . _ _ _ _ _ _ . .

Lifting the hat of Knowledge onto the statue.

Death of Ku'uku'u.

Chapter 2: . _ _ _ _ _ _ _ .

Dances preceding the work of sculpture.

Feast after the sculpture has been finished.

Chapter 3: . _ _ _ _ _ _ _ .

Fecundation

Announcement of the birth of a child.

Chapter 5: . _ _ _ _ _ _ _ _ _ .

·Roots,

trunk and foliage.

The *moai kava-kava* statuary is made from the trunk of the *toro miro* tree.

Chapter 6: . _ _ _ _ _ .

Hiva.

Transporting the statues.

The statues were taken to the edge of the sea, where they stood with their backs to Hiva (see also the second line in Chapter 6: the statue will be the receptacle of *mana*).

Chapter 10: . . . .

Current of life animating the statues.	Long-Ears possessing knowledge of that life of the statues.

Finally, let us note that sometimes a line can be read from one end to the other, from left to right or right to left, but that in other cases, depending on the time or place of the action, the signs are arranged differently in relation to the central theme. Chapter 4 illustrates this particularly well.

CHAPTER THIRTEEN
Ancestor Worship

To interpret this line of ideograms, the last one on the page of lines from the Tomenika manuscript shown at the beginning of this book, we will need to use nearly all the "keys" to *rongo-rongo* writing given so far.

It is important to elucidate the meaning of the central theme:

and the end signs:

We must note the association of six signs, taken in pairs, with a new symbol:

Finally, we must recall a certain number of ideograms that we have previously encountered.

For a better understanding of what follows, I will now give the general meaning of the line: it deals with worship of the Great Ancestors, their origin and the various manifestations by which the Easter Islanders invoked them.

In studying this series of ideograms we must determine the meaning of each of them before reconstructing the whole line, in the fullness of its meaning.

The three signs represent the spirit, in the Easter Island sense of *aku-aku*. Each being has its spirit, its immaterial double; on Easter Island, the *aku-aku* is also the presence of a dead person's spirit. We will recall the legend in Chapter 5, where the demon appeared in this form, with his forked head: . Chapter 10: "The Long-Ears knew demons and the spirits called *aku-akus*," represented by this sign: .

The upper part of all these signs is the same:

But the general representation of an *aku-aku* in

rongo-rongo writing does not, properly speaking have a head.

In the legend of the seven explorers we have already seen this absence of a head in representations of a spirit:

.  . The spirit turtle (Chapter 1).

.  . The spirit of Hau Maka, in the lower left part (Chapter 1).

The *aku-aku* is symbolized by this "ectoplasmic" flame  in which only the upper part has the forked aspect of a demon, without a body or head.

.  This sign, at the extreme right of the line, implies two meanings; one is indicated by its form, the other by its position.

a) The form expresses speech, as a ribbon coming from a mouth. We have encountered this several times before:

The "bird's cry" on the island of Motu Nui, to announce the name of the man who will become the birdman (Chapter 4).

The cry uttered by Prince Rokoroko Hetau when he was born (Chapter 12).

The first word (Chapter 11: creation of the world).

. . "There came a white bird . . . It cried, 'Kuihi-Kuaha' " (Chapter 11).

. . Crowing of the cock, announcing the birth of a child (Chapter 3).

In ancient Chinese writing, speech is indicated by a speaking mouth; that is, a mouth emitting air, which is visible in winter. The idea is the same in Easter Island writing.

Speech is here coming from a mouth in the shape of a circle , which thus corresponds to *mana*. The "head" has ears. The sign designates the sacred word, the word of the Ancestors.

b) The position of the sign indicates that those Ancestors came from the west. With two apparent exceptions which we will consider later, all signs containing the idea of the origin of the Easter Islanders, the Polynesians who descended from Hotu Matua and therefore had their origin in Hiva, or the west in general, appear on the right side of a line and are oriented toward the right if they indicate motion toward the original homeland.

. . The spirit turtle returns to Hiva.

. . The cock crows toward Hiva to announce the birth of a child.

. . The "head" of the symbol of life is turned toward Hiva (Chapter 13).

They are oriented toward the left, however, even though they are still on the right side of the line, if they express motion away from Hiva, or simply a point of departure in the west.

. "His current of life, starting from Hiva . . ." (Chapter 1).

. Symbol of death: moving away from Hiva (Chapter 1).

. The seven explorers; the two small lines at the top mark their original attachment to Hiva, from which they departed (Chapter 1).

Two signs seem to be exceptions to this rule  (Chapter 6) and  (Chapter 12).

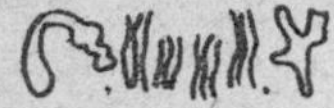

(Chapter 6) The statue has its back to the sea, beyond which is the emblem of Hiva. This sign 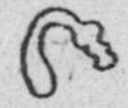 is oriented toward the right, but it is at the left end of the line. Its position reveals a hidden meaning that we have already discussed: all the Easter Island statues face away from their sculptors' original homeland.

There is no way to know whether this statue seen in profile  is from the first or the second period. To make it a symbol of the statues of both periods, Tomenika placed this sign  at the left end of the line and oriented it toward the right: the statue of the second period faces away from Hiva, whose emblem is turned toward the right, but the statue of the first period faces away from South America, for the sign is at the left end of the line and thus indicates the east, if we assume that beyond its meaning of Hiva, this sign expresses the general idea of the original homeland.

Pursuing our analysis, we have the impression that this is not merely a hypothesis, but is clearly indicated in the manuscript.

This ideogram represents Hiva (see Chapter 6), but also the original homeland of the Easter Islanders.

The Easter Island statues face away from their sculptors' homeland:

—The statues of the first period face away from South America.

—The statues of the second period face away from Hiva.

In Chapter 6 I interpreted these two signs . . , not separated by punctuation, as follows:

The statue is seen from the front and in profile, facing away from the sea . . , beyond which is Hiva .

But aside from this interpretation involving the

ideas of front and profile, we see that Tomenika expressed the second meaning by "writing" a statue from each of the two periods:

Statue of the first period, with tapered base.

Statue of the second period, with convex base.

We have already seen similar representations in the second line of Chapter 6:

Statue of the second period.

Statue of the first period.

. . In this case Tomenika had to show only one of the two statues facing away from the sea, and not the other, since the homeland of the first-period sculptors was in the opposite direction from that of the second-period sculptors. That is what he did, but he did not separate the two signs by punctuation and he placed the mark of the original land beyond the sea . . in relation to these two signs . .

Tomenika did the same thing in the second line in Chapter 6: he showed a statue of the first period from the front and one from the second period in profile  without separating them by punctuation.

To return to apparent anomalies of orientation in certain *rongo-rongo* signs, I will mention this other exception:

(Chapter 12) The bird that was to go back to Hiva is oriented toward the left; but that is because Tomenika wanted to show that before going back to Hiva, the bird first had to have come from it, for that is the meaning of the sentence spoken on that occasion: "Go, return to Hiva."

After that long digression I will point out that the sign I had begun considering  , comes from the right, from the west, and appears at the right end of the line. So there is no ambiguity in its expression of an origin west of Easter Island.

. To understand this ideogram we must recall two others:

(Chapter 1) Lifting the hat of Knowledge on a ramp of ropes .

(Chapter 1) Death: "one of the lines is birth, the other is death. Between the two is life."

The Easter Islanders and the Polynesians recited

genealogical lists of their ancestors, using knotted cords, with each knot corresponding to the name of a known ancestor. (The use of such knotted cords was common in South America, where they were called *quipus*, but they were used for a different purpose: counting.)

. The meaning is now apparent: along two cords are knots, each one evoking an ancestor, and the cords form the two lines that are sufficient to express a life.

In this line, the birdman is a symbol of the man of Easter Island.

Finally, two signs seem new to us:

I will put off the surprise of discovering them in the general context of the line we are going to translate. Interpretation will be oriented around the three central ideograms: .

To the left the birdman , and therefore the man of Easter Island, invokes his ancestor .

The ancestor bears the circle of *mana*. This is the first and only time that this symbol of Knowledge appears on a birdman. I have already pointed out that a representation of the birdman, shown with the head of a bird (evoking Make-Make, the god of birds), was enough to express Knowledge, with no need to add the circle of *mana*.

We have seen that signs depicting a symbol *in profile*, whether it be a symbol of a statue or of a person, and even if it carries the meaning of initiation or Knowledge, almost never have the circle.

In Chapter 6, these two associated signs .

show the statue from the front  with the circle, but

in profile  without it.

It is the same in Chapter 1:  symbol of death;

and in Chapter 3:  symbol of life.

All previous representations of the birdman are seen in profile and do not bear the specific mark of *mana*:

(Chapter 2)  (Chapter 5)

(Chapter 4) 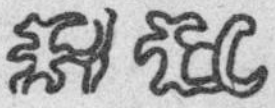 (Chapter 9)

The one we are now considering  . is an exception because it represents the Great Ancestor. Here, the head is larger than in other representations of the birdman. It is comparable to that of the ideo-

gram to the right of it . .

This sign is a dragon. Ancient Chinese signs depicting dragons, dating from the tenth century B.C. have been found carved on tortoise shells. Here are three of them:  . Their resemblance to the Easter Island sign  is obvious.

The Great Ancestor  whom the birdman seems to be invoking, with the dragon between them, is *the Asian ancestor*.

Here is a translation of the whole line:

.  There came the ancestral Word, a sacred Word spoken by a mouth that was not that of Knowledge. It bears ears—"The first race had large ears"—and came from the west.

.  . Came from Asia, where the land of elephants was. (Ancient Chinese:  elephant. The Chinese sign is shown to indicate that pictographs were used in both cases.)

.  . The first three ancestors came:

.  . The Great Ancestor, the god, with the head of the bird-dragon .

. . . The first man, and his spirit . .

. . The first woman, and her spirit  . , which bears the circle of Knowledge, for the concept of motherhood was sacred and divine. (Compare the symbol of fecundation  in Chapter 3. These two signs are clearly similar.)

From these ancestors came the man  and the woman  of Easter Island. They united  and mingled their two spirits  . This sign has two upper parts, denoting the fusion of the two spirits   , and a prolonged lower part  which indicates a woman  , as we have already seen.

The man invoked his ancestors and their spirits.

He invoked them with chants to the glory of the received ancestral Word  .

He invoked them by the composition of string figures, held in his hand.

He invoked them by incantatory dances.

His three ancestors and their spirits

the god

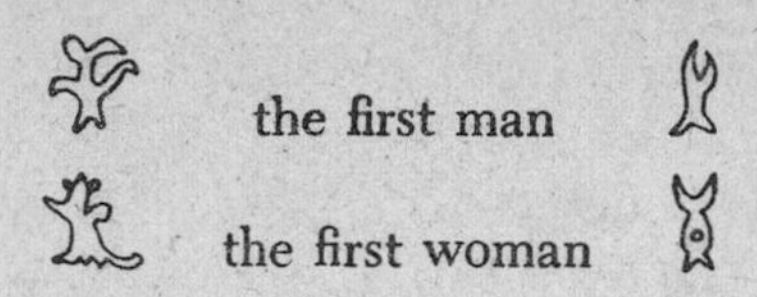

Three was Knowledge. His three ancestors, who lived west of him, in the land of Asia.

CHAPTER FOURTEEN

Origin of the Easter Islanders

The origin of the Easter Islanders is one of the most fascinating problems, but also one of the hardest to solve.

With regard to the people discovered on the island by Europeans in the eighteenth century, things seem simple, but the simplicity is only apparent.

They were pure Polynesians, speaking a Polynesian language. Yet among them were very tall, red-haired people with European features, comparable to those who lived in South America before the Incas. No Easter Islanders had Mongoloid features. No statue on the island has slanted eyes.

The origin of those Polynesians lay toward the west. The Marquesas Islands? The Gambier Islands? There are certain points in common among the Marquesas, the Gambiers and Easter Island. The Easter Island language is a branch of a Polynesian language; there are *ahus* in the Marquesas, and priests called *rongo-rongos*. But the statues and the writing belong exclusively to Easter Island.

The Hiva Archipelago, with its two islands of Marae Renga which appear in the legends of both Easter Island and the Gambiers, may have been part of that Polynesian island group, but with one special feature: the writing that King Hotu Matua is said to have brought to Easter Island, inscribed on banana leaves. Are we to assume, in view of similarities with Chinese writing, that the *rongo-rongo* signs were transmitted to Marae Renga at the time of an Asian influence? If so, that influence must have taken place at a time when the Marquesas were populated only partially and in an unorganized manner, since there was no writing there. Or did Hotu Matua's own ancestors come from a more distant land to the west?

Rongo-rongo writing, transcribed by Polynesians, places the origin of the Great Ancestors in a land to the west, indicated by symbols of the elephant and the dragon, which are purely Asian. None of the Easter Islanders had Mongoloid features, yet the similarities between Chinese writing and Easter Island writing seem undeniable, though there is one consistent difference, which may not be significant: the double contours of *rongo-rongo* characters. Here is an illustration of what I mean by "double contours":

Easter Island: [glyph] Swallow.

China: [glyph] Swallow.

Moreover, the two writings developed in quite different directions. Easter Island writing moved toward perfection in figurative representation, conditioned by total dependence on mythology, which gave it such a specific imprint that it became an absolutely unique form of writing.

Finally, in China changes in writing were partially related to use of the brush, but on Easter Island the technique remained unaltered: scribes went on carving their characters into wood. In view of this, and the fact that Easter Island was an isolated world, the apparent stagnation of *rongo-rongo* writing is understandable. It is almost unnecessary to add that it belonged exclusively to a privileged class which allowed no changes to be made in it.

What are we to think of those tall, red-haired people with European features? When the Spaniards first arrived in the Incan Empire they encountered tall, long-headed people with white skin and European features. They were told that these were the last survivors of the race that had preceded the Incas. It was they who were said to have built the city of Tiahuanaco.

Tiahuanaco flourished between the seventh and twelfth centuries; radioactive carbon datings place construction of the Ahu Vinapu in the eighth century. Since the Spaniards were also white, the Incas thought the first race had returned and they therefore put up no resistance, which was fatal to them. What are we to think of the pre-Incan architecture of the Ahu Vinapu, which recalls certain walls found in Peru? What are we to conclude from the fact that the Easter Island kings were dolichocephalic, while the farther west one goes, toward Hiva, the more the people become brachycephalic?

The difficulty of understanding Easter Island lies in

the fact that, on the basis of concrete evidence, we can ask questions which seem to call for contradictory answers, in both ancient and recent times.

From the writing, it appears that the original homeland was west of Easter Island. I believe we can say that the writing came from a place west of Hiva. But what about the people and the statuary? Legends say that the first race came from a land behind America and brought *rongo-rongo* writing with them, and that the only other place where that writing exists is in Asia.

Legends and *rongo-rongo* texts both refer to Asia. What, then, is the meaning of "a land behind America"? Must we assume, without prejudging the routes followed by the successive migrations to Matakiterani (Easter Island), that the notions of east and west, with regard to Asia, have only a relative value on Easter Island? Since Asia, mentioned by both texts and legends, is practically at the antipodes of Easter Island, it can quite legitimately be said to lie either east or west of the island. This viewpoint is especially valid in relation to a concept of the Pacific as it was seen by peoples living on the islands and continents at its edges: a concept that made it a world in itself.

There are two theories with regard to the route followed by the migrations.

At present the general tendency is to reject the possibility of civilization having been brought to Easter Island from the east; that is, from South America. The fragile balsa rafts of the Amerindians are not considered adequate for such a voyage. But the other theory, that of Thor Heyerdahl, maintains that there was an influence from the east. Heyerdahl's best supporting evidence is the fact that he himself made a similar Pacific voyage on his famous balsa raft, the *Kon-Tiki*. The difficulties of traveling from South America to Easter Island on a raft are very real; because of them, we can speak of a "bringing of civilization" only insofar as a small number of people may have reached the island against all odds.

It was not the same with the Polynesians who came from Hiva. They had impressive double boats that enabled them to travel all over the Pacific. Moreover, the legend of King Anua Motua says that he left from Mangareva, reached Tierra del Fuego and finally came to Easter Island. The Polynesians left their homeland for known reasons. The first was usually the outcome of a tribal war: when a king had been defeated, to save his honor—and this possibility was left open to him by his victorious rival—he had to go off with his people in search of a new home. This is mentioned in the legend of King Hotu Matua. But it is also said that his original homeland Hiva, called Marae Renga, was submerged at the time of a cataclysm. Many arguments, which we will consider later, seem to support this latter reason.

But we have the impression that although Easter Island could be reached in one way or another, leaving it was problematical or even impossible. When a group of people had wandered over the sea for a seemingly endless time and had then been saved from death only by having come upon that isolated little island, they must have had no desire to set off on another voyage like the one that had ended safely only by a miracle.

It seems that Easter Island, the Navel of the

World, was a center of incoming currents but never a source of outgoing ones; its writing is unique in the whole Pacific area and its statues have given it such an original character that it has become one of the most fascinating places in the world. It received elements from great and ancient civilizations, and then, after the initial impact, it developed those elements in its own distinctive way. But it gave nothing. How could it have exported anything, since it was the world's most isolated place?

I believe we can reach partial conclusions on the following "cultural" points:

—The first inspiration for the statues was given by people who came from South America. The architecture of the Ahu Vinapu is almost undeniable proof of this, and so is that need to erect gigantic statues, a tendency not found in the rest of Polynesia, or at least not on such a scale.

—The writing shows clear evidence of Asian, and especially Chinese, influence. Since it is found nowhere else in the Polynesian islands, and since it was brought to Easter Island by Hotu Matua, we must assume that this influence was exercised in a land—Hiva, and Marae Renga in particular—which later disappeared, at a time before the rest of the Marquesas or Gambier Islands were thoroughly populated.

Here a difficulty arises. Radioactive carbon datings show the presence of human beings in the Marquesas as early as 150 B.C. According to the royal genealogies preserved on Easter Island, Hotu Matua arrived there in the twelfth century A.D. Were there omissions in those genealogies? Considering the influence of Chinese characters on *rongo-rongo* writing, that twelfth-century date for Hotu Matua's arrival seems too late. And since legends specifically say that the statues of the first period were already there when he arrived, the time of that period should also be moved back. We must bear in mind that the statues of the second period have a degenerate style in relation to the earlier ones that remained at the foot of the Rano Raraku volcano. But the major argument seems to be that the Marquesas were already populated in the twelfth century, yet nothing comparable to *rongo-rongo* writing was found there.

To sum up, Easter Island received writing from the west and statuary from the east, but it gave nothing: its writing did not return to Polynesia and the distinctive style of its statues did not inspire any of the sculptors of the pre-Incan and Incan cities.

I must point out that when I say that the statuary came from the east, I am referring only to the technique of making it. Did the form of the faces, which gives the statues their originality, also come from the east, like their long fingernails and the inscriptions on their backs? I will speak of India later in this chapter, but if there was an influence that extended from India to Hiva, we can reasonably expect to find traces of it between those two places. Katherine Routledge reported that this aspect of the faces of the Easter Island statues closely resembled the carved prows of certain boats in the Solomon Islands, in Melanesia, which is on the route from India to Polynesia. The British ethnographer Balfour also noticed certain similarities between Melanesia and Easter Island, aside from the form of the statues' facial features.

Alfred Métraux, however, seems to reject any connection between those two civilizations, and P.H. Buck maintains that waves of eastward migration from southeast Asia would have passed through Micronesia, rather than Melansia, before reaching Polynesia.

Opinion is thus divided with regard to the route followed by migrations from the west which first came to Hiva, then went on to Easter Island. I will nevertheless adopt the hypothesis that contact between an ethic from the west and a technology from the east was required in order to produce the stone giants of Easter Island, and that they acquired their special character from the interaction between those two elements.

But what about the people of Easter Island? Legend says that the people of the first race had large ears, brought a form of writing found elsewhere only in Asia, and formerly lived on two Polynesian islands. Marae Renga?

This first race arrived long before Hotu Matua, yet writing and Asia are already associated with them.

I have pointed out the relativity of the position of Asia in relation to Easter Island: east and west can both be legitimately considered in interpreting the legends.

We have returned to the subject of Asia. I am not seeking spectacular, unexpected revelations, however. I am simply inviting the reader to follow a line of inquiry that is difficult but opens onto fabulous perspectives.

China, which I have mentioned so often, is not the only part of Asia where writing with similarities to that of Easter Island can be found. And since there is no evidence of Mongoloid features in either the people or the statues of Easter Island, we must look for a region of Asia where the people do not have slanted eyes, where elephants live (see Chapter 13), and where there is a form of writing that shows similarities to *rongo-rongo* signs. That brings us to a consideration of the neolithic writing of the cities of Mohenjo-Daro and Harappa, in the Indus Valley; it is said to date from 2500 B.C. The seals of those cities, on which the writing was inscribed, were made of soapstone. Let us recall once again that, according to Easter Island legend, the first race brought a form of writing that was engraved on stone and found elsewhere only in Asia.

The table on page 164 shows Mohenjo-Daro signs, as published by Guillaume de Hevesy, with an Easter Island sign beside each of them. We can compare only shapes here, not meanings. The *rongo-rongo* signs do not appear in the Tomenika manuscript, which I have till now considered exclusively, but are taken from wooden tablets, and no definitive meaning can be assigned to an isolated character, taken out of its context. Some of them, however, are similar to others that we already know.

The resemblances between the Mohenjo-Daro and Easter Island signs are quite clear. Are we to conclude that the western origin of Hotu Matua's ancestors was in the Indus Valley? That would mean accepting this assertion, quoted by Métraux: "In Asia there was a common center from which whole peoples migrated toward the Pacific, taking with them, according to some authors, the ancient pre-Columbian civilizations." Would that be valid for all Easter

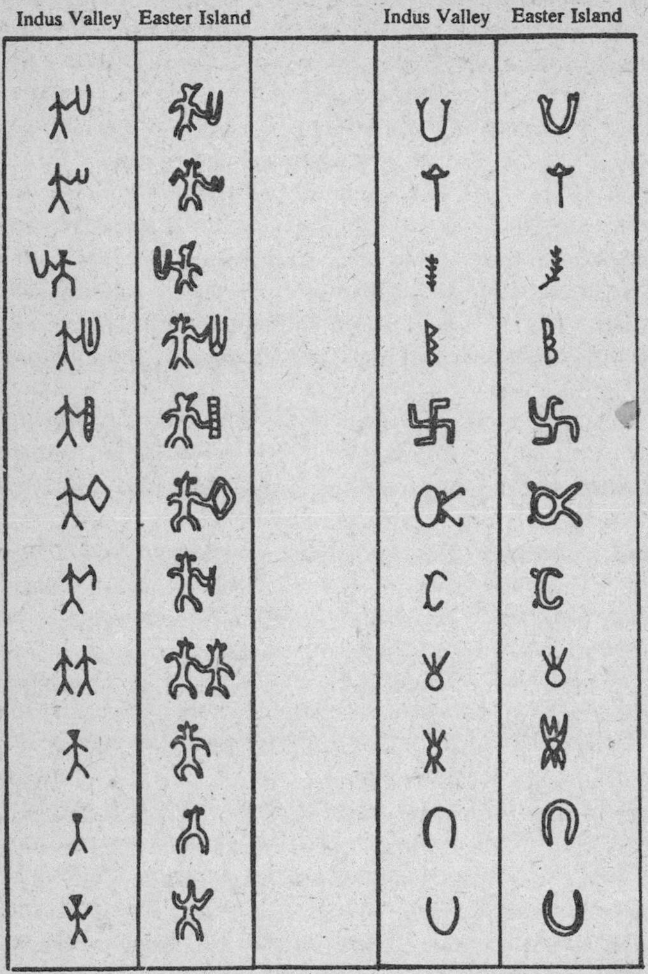

Indus Valley	Easter Island		Indus Valley	Easter Island

Islanders? And for those who made the statues of the first period?

An essential element seems to be lacking between Easter Island and Asia. The writing exists in Asia and on Easter Island, but nowhere in Polynesia, from where Hotu Matua came. We are forced to think increasingly of that vanished archipelago: Hiva.

Legend says that the first race formerly lived on two Polynesian islands. Hiva surely underwent an Asian, Chinese influence, but kept a distinctive anthropological character. In fact, Hiva was probably as distinctive as Easter Island later became. The Asian influence had been exercised there long before Hotu Matua, and long before him there had already been contacts between Hiva and Easter Island, as seems to be indicated by the signs on the backs of the statues of the first period, and the special shape of their hands with long, tapering fingernails.

But will we ever know Hiva unless it suddenly becomes possible to translate the ancient *rongo-rongo* tablets? Meanwhile Hiva appears to be a necessity in understanding Easter Island.

As for the bringing of civilization, including the statues, from the east, legends also refer to a point of departure farther to the east, a "land behind America," in which Asia is still involved. If those people originated in Asia, why is there no writing similar to that of Easter Island in the pre-Columbian civilizations? There are pictographic systems in South America—among the Cuna Indians of Panama, for example—in which certain signs are comparable to *rongo-rongo* characters, but such similarities are of little significance if they involve only images of concrete realities: different peoples may depict such things as rain and the sun by means of simple drawings which resemble each other but imply no common origin.

That is why we may think that a phenomenon of space distortion took place in the legend. In the first period on Easter Island there may have been a fusion between the populations that came from the east and the west. From that union the great statues were born. Later the fusion was so complete that the people of the second migration, from Hiva, may have attributed a common origin to their predecessors, even though they knew they had come to Easter Island from two different directions. In any case this hypothesis reinforces the view that the dorsal signs and long fingernails of the statues had their origin in the west, having been brought by the first migration from Hiva, which I have called the "Asian" migration.

Or the legend may be accurate; but that would not rule out the two preceding hypotheses.

I will now consider the problem of an eastern origin in the same way as that of a western origin.

I have said, "China is not the only part of Asia . . ." I will now say that Tiahuanaco, on the shore of Lake Titicaca, in Bolivia, is not the only cradle of all the pre-Columbian civilizations. To remain in agreement with Easter Island legend, we must try to find traces of a South American civilization that meets one criterion: showing a conclusive similarity, of any kind, to Asia.

This is fundamental, because otherwise we might try to compare diverse statues and architectures, as we did with the Ahu Vinapu and pre-Incan walls. In that case the resemblance was obvious, but did it involve consequences that gave Easter Island its full significance? Here, too, we seem to lack an essential element, like Hiva in the case of the west.

In the west, the original culture may have left from India, passed through Melanesia and taken root in Polynesia, in Hiva. There, the second Chinese influence on *rongo-rongo* writing may have made itself felt.

In the east, for the moment, we have found only one influence: that of the tall, red-haired people with European features. From them came the inspiration of the Ahu Vinapu, and a contribution to the technique of making the great statues. (Till now I have neglected to say, since it seemed so natural to me, that those red-haired people had elongated earlobes.) And legend says that they brought a writing found nowhere else but in Asia.

In order for there to be harmony, and I feel that necessity, there must be a second element, farther back in time. In reference to the first race, legend speaks of other people who came from a land behind America.

To find a trace in South America of that first race mentioned by Easter Island legends, we must find a civilization marked by a purely Asian imprint. That is the guiding thread.

Look at the two drawings on page 168. They were made on the basis of photographs published in *L'Art ancien de l'Amérique du Sud*, by François Hébert-Stevens and Claude Arthaud. They represent monolithic statues discovered in South America.

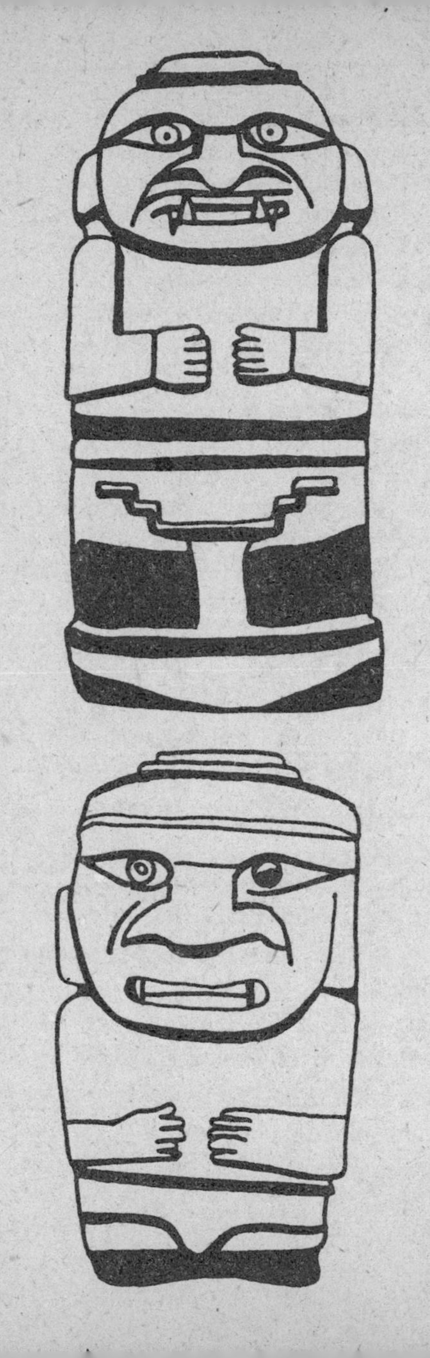

Look closely at their eyes. The same eyes appear on certain ancient Chinese vases.

Furthermore their ears are long. The hands are placed over the belly. The head is surmounted by a protuberance. These "cat-toothed" statues were placed inside temples made of flat stones.

The statue improperly called the "Wave Breaker" was found at Orongo, on Easter Island, in a similarly built stone house.

Other statues guard the temple on the outside. "They are armed with a club carried on one shoulder," writes Hébert-Stevens, "recalling the *lokapalas* which guard the entrances of Buddhist temples in India and China."

These statues are of different types. Some have a triangular head, and we will recall the triangular-headed statue of an old man on Easter Island, from the earliest period. Others have perfectly round eyes. Still others resemble sculptured columns, with the arms over the belly, like the sculptured column found on Easter Island by Heyerdahl, also from the earliest period.

At that extraordinary site in South America, probably the oldest and largest, more than three hundred stone giants stand in an area of several square miles, some of them more than twelve feet tall.

We are far away from Tiahuanaco, in time and space. Carbon-14 datings situate the site in the sixth century B.C. Tiahuanaco may have come into being at some time around the beginning of the Christian era, before reaching its full development several centuries later.

There is a mystery in that fantastic place: "We

know nothing about the people who transported and carved those enormous monoliths and built those temples, nor do we know how their culture disappeared," writes Hébert-Stevens.

And writing? Graphic signs are found there: circles, squares, crosses. Their repetition might seem to indicate that they are hieroglyphics. That is all we know.

But might those signs not be the most important symbols of the original writing? If the people who made them were the first to reach Easter Island in the earliest period, those fundamental signs make it legitimate to say that they brought writing. If that civilization had initially come from Asia, bringing those primary characters, they had not evolved because they had not received, as in the case of Hiva, a second stimulus that would have conditioned their development.

That place in South America was one of the major crossroads of civilization on the continent. It is called San Agustin and it is in Colombia.

What does the legend mean when it says, "They came from a land behind America?" Are we to understand that they originated on the other side of the Atlantic, in Europe or Africa, and then went to Asia? In ancient times, were the whole Pacific Ocean and its shores regarded as a universe. If so, should we invoke the idea of antipodes here, as we have done elsewhere? Does "behind South America" mean "toward the far north"? If the migration from India to Hiva passed by way of the south, did this one, starting from the same place, pass by way of the north, across the Bering Strait of the Aleutian Islands? Were the people of San Agustin distant descendants of the first inhabitants of America who came from Asia by that route? Yellow people with blond hair, says the legend. Certain people in Asia have blond hair, and so do certain mummies in South America. As they were crossing China on their way to the Bering Strait, after having left from the common center in Asia, did they encounter people with slanted eyes, whose image they continued to remember?

Are those two races—one of a "European" type, the other Mongoloid—reflected in the two kinds of statues at San Agustin: those with round eyes and those with slanted eyes?

The chronology of events and the datings at San Agustin are another argument that makes me believe that dates of all the Easter Island periods must be pushed back. The earliest period, usually situated in the fourth century B.C., may actually have occurred before then, and we have already considered other reasons for assuming that the first and second periods were earlier than is generally thought.

From San Agustin those people went to Easter Island, where they made contact with those who came from Hiva, long before Hotu Matua.

What came of that reunion between two groups who had left from the same place in Asia and then met again after having traveled in different directions? In the "anguish of the island," between the silence of the sky and the roar of the ocean, there was an affirmation of unity.

The principle of the monolithic statuary was preserved, as at San Agustin. The inscriptions on the backs of the statues, fundamental signs expressing elements of the universe, were adopted without reserve because they came from the original homeland. That incredible meeting could not have failed to engender a need for a return to worship of the common ancestors. The statues were consecrated to it.

That worship had to be permanent and undivided. The principle of varied statues, as at San Agustin, was abandoned, and statues in the style of the earliest period—the triangular-headed old man, the rectangular column with arms, etc.—were no longer made. From now on there would be only "figurative" statues. There would be only a statuary of the ancestors, single and whole, like the thought that inspired it; all the statues on Easter Island would have the same appearance, the same form, the same face.

At this point the people looked at each other. What kind of eyes should they give their statues: round or slanted? At San Agustin there were both. In their ancient wisdom they arrived at a new "Solomon's judgment": the statues would have no eyes. Those that stand at the foot of the volcano have only deep eye sockets, opened and closed by the sun.

Another point was settled: the hands of the statues. They would remain under the navel because that was of prime importance, as we will see; but, from the land of Asia, they would have tapering fingernails.

Time had to pass; the two groups had to become a people capable of achieving what they wanted to do. Time passed.

Then came the red-haired people, who may have been other descendants of the San Agustin people. From Peru they brought knowledge and technology and gave new impetus to the urge to make stone come alive, as the Chinese influence had given new impetus to *rongo-rongo* writing in Hiva. Everything was ready. Now that the people were finally united and numerous, anything was possible.

This first period had to be gigantic, in keeping with the dimensions of their history and their thought . . .

Immense statues stood at the foot of Rano Raraku, facing westward.

At first I stated hypotheses based on an "instantaneous" vision of things. That method led me to conclusions which reflected an initial approach to events, but those events also appeared instantaneous, like photographs taken at one specific moment. To formulate other opinions, I had to go beyond that framework and, alongside an overall view, reinsert all those hypotheses in a dynamic context closer to the movement of history.

Perhaps I can now propose that overall view of Easter Island. Like builders removing their scaffolding when the house is finished, let us look at the conclusions that present themselves to us.

Except for the disappearance of Hiva, which was relatively sudden, and except for the "statue-overthrowing time," which did not last long, only about half a century, it is hard to imagine that Easter Island civilization was always shaken by upheavals so violent as to place everything in question. We have the impression that, preceded by his seven legendary explorers, Hotu Matua found the island deserted, except for the great statues and certain *ahus*. If so, this would indicate a complete break between the first and second periods.

What happened earlier to bring about the extinction of the preceding civilization? Could there have been another cataclysm? No. There is no trace of a geological catastrophe on the island at that time. The explanation is simply that the legend naturally focuses on Hotu Matua and says little about the survival of the people who lived on the island before him, because otherwise how could we explain the presence of those red-haired people whose descendants were still on the island in the eighteenth century, and who did not come with Hotu Matua?

Envisaging a complete discontinuity between the different periods of the island's history corresponds to what I have called "instantaneous hypotheses," conceived simply as a means of investigation.

Between the end of the first period and Hotu Matua's arrival, which marked the beginning of the second period, there may have been continuity, for reasons that I will give later.

It seems even clearer that there was a connection, even a fusion, between the preceding periods: the earliest period from the east and the "Asian" period from Hiva. The arrival of the red-haired people from Peru determined the development of the first period, with the great statues. But first there had to be the time necessary for the formation of a people. They had to become accustomed to statuary again, and before undertaking the stone giants they had to begin by making smaller statues, like the ones Francis Mazière found in his excavations of Rano Raraku. Then time passed while the great statues were being made, as it had passed while the people were learning to speak the same language.

In the outline I will give below, dates are hard to establish, for reasons that I have mentioned several times, but the order of events seems easier to establish.

In the west

—Departure from a common Asian center: perhaps the Indus Valley.

—Passage through Melanesia.

—Settlement in Polynesia, in Hiva.

—Chinese influence on Hiva.

—Two migrations from Hiva: first, the "Asian" period which, by its fusion with the earliest Easter Island period, contributed to the development of the first period; and then Hotu Matua's arrival, which began the second period.

In the east

—Migration to Easter Island by the people of San Agustin, whose remote ancestors had perhaps left from the "common center in Asia." Beginning of the earliest period.

—Second migration from South America by people who preceded the Incas. They came from Peru, perhaps from Tiahuanaco. They joined the two cultures already existing on the island. Beginning of the first period.

The style of the Ahu Vinapu (convex slabs, beveled corners, stones with projecting edges fitting into stones with receding edges) is characteristic of a style that preceded what was to become the architecture of the walls of all the Incan cities. The inspiration of the Ahu Vinapu could only have come from South America. Rejecting the possibility of any South American influence on Easter Island, as is often done at present, amounts to purely and simply denying the existence of the Ahu Vinapu; yet it is there, with its length of more than two hundred and fifty feet. This type of monument exists only in South America and on Easter Island, and nowhere else in the whole western Pacific.

Some scientists maintain that influence on Easter Island has come only from west of it. If so, since the design and construction of the Ahu Vinapu are found nowhere west of the island, those scientists would have to say that they were developed in Hiva. But it would be contrary to their habits to support a hypothesis with the idea of a vanished archipelago. Furthermore the design of the Ahu Vinapu did not come from Hiva, and I have given reasons for believing that it came from the east. A monument is always built by people. In this case the people had red hair, European features, tall stature, etc.

In the interpretation of *rongo-rongo* writing that I have given, this double current of influence, from the east and from the west, is clearly indicated. The following signs from Chapter 6 are particularly important in this regard:

The first-period statue with a tapered base faces away from the sea, beyond which is the original homeland of its sculptors that is, South Amer-

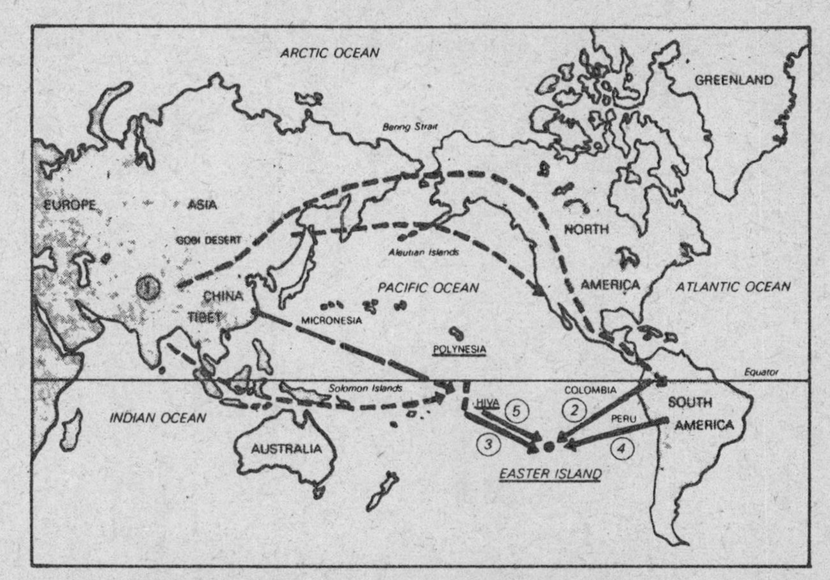

1. Departure from a common center in Asia: Indus Valley? 2. San Agustin: earliest period. 3. Hiva: "Asian" period. 4. Tiahuanaco: first period. 5. Hotu Matua: second period.

ica, since *the position of this sign* [glyph] *at the left end of the line indicates the east.*

The second-period statue with a convex base [glyph] receives its *mana* from the original homeland of its sculptors; that is, from Hiva [glyph], which is beyond the sea, since the sign of the homeland [glyph] *is oriented toward the right, indicating the west.*

Easter Island became the "universal receptacle in which two civilizations, having left from a common point and traveled over the globe in opposite directions, were fused at that "Navel of the World."

I will leave the conclusion of these last few pages to Alfred Métraux:

"If, in all of Polynesia, only the inhabitants of that 'Ultima Thule' knew the art of writing, and if they alone were able to make and erect the great statues, they were entitled to proclaim themselves the representatives of a grandiose past, and the sons of a privileged race."

I am prevented from developing this chapter further by the disappearance of Hiva, in which I believe, and by the fact that the ancient *rongo-rongo* texts have not yet been translated. But I am eager to return to the similarities between the writings of China and Easter Island because they may show the reader a new path toward discovery of Easter Island, and they may also provide him with unexpected elements, some of which seem amazing to me. First, however, let us take one last look at these three signs:

Mohenjo-Daro

China

Easter Island

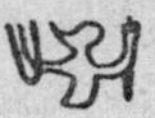

They are symbols of Knowledge.

Since I have mentioned Mohenjo-Daro, I will point out that in Sanskrit, the sacred language of India, the word for "spirit" is *mana*.

CHAPTER FIFTEEN

The Deep Meaning of the *Rongo-Rongo* Signs

I began this book with a hypothesis concerning the transportation of the statues. Then, assuming that *rongo-rongo* writing would necessarily deal with that subject, I looked for the ideogram corresponding to my hypothesis, which can be expressed as follows:

I found this Easter Island sign in the same line as the advancing statue, a short distance away from it .

Then I gave my interpretation of those two hundred and fifty ideograms, linked to each other in each line by a context related to known, precise Easter Island traditions. Only after I have given them meaning did I study their similarities to ancient Chinese characters. With growing excitement, I saw that in a number of cases the main meaning of an archaic Chinese sign* was in perfect agreement with the second, deeper meaning that could be attributed to the corresponding Easter Island sign.

We have seen the master sculptor who drew the outline of the future statue on the stone. Through the square he holds, there is an evocation of work, action and builders that could only have come from Chinese thought. Since the square also implies the earth, the coexistence of those two symbols forms a whole which is in harmony with the statues of Easter Island, endowed with life and *mana*, in union with the universe.

In Chapter 7, comparing the two writings, we saw some astonishing similarities:

Sound: China

Easter

Upward motion: China

Easter

Here, we may be going beyond morphological comparison, but we will begin with the simplest analogies, in the immediate sense of the term.

China: Newborn child.

*The ancient Chinese signs and their interpretations are taken from Leon Wieger, *op. cit.*

Easter:  Symbol of life being embodies in the newborn child.

China:  Son, child whose fontanels are open.

Easter:  Statue of a child, with open fontanels (see the legend of Rokoroko Hetau).

China: Concept of Union.

Easter:  Head of a child (Chapter 3); assemblage of skull bones, and perhaps union of the head and *mana*.

China:  Oviduct and ovaries.

Easter:  Oviduct and egg. (I have already explained the oblique line across the egg. It is found on the ovary in Chinese writing.)

China: Woman. *The right-hand part is elongated.*

Initially the sign was symmetrical but scribes altered it to avoid the effort of having to draw a sign with two identical parts.

Easter:  Woman giving the sculptor the crown of ferns.  The woman ancestor. Umbilical cord evoking the origin of woman and the divinities.

China: The three powers: heaven, earth and mankind.

These three lines, drawn vertically, are part of the sign , indicating an influence from above.

Sign by which heaven instructs mankind.

This sign represents what hangs in the sky; that is, the sun, the moon and the stars, whose changes reveal transcendent things to man.

Easter: Signs on the backs of the statues. In the first place, they are symbols of the elements of the universe. Perhaps we should add, "elements of the universe, which reveal transcendent things to man." We will see later that there is reason to believe this, judging from the position in which the signs are inscribed on the backs of the statues.

China: Plants, particularly herbaceous plants. The repetition expresses their multiplicity.

Easter: On the little islands of Motu Nui and Motu Iti (see Chapter 4), plants are represented , two on each island, to show their multiplicity.

The same idea appears in Chapter 2. Several sculptors were needed for each statue. The writing shows two: . . . (See also Chapter 6: several ropes .)

Chapter 9, on the transmission of the writing, will enable us to go further in research of these analogies.

China: The first memory aid invented after knotted cords: notches cut into a slat | or small board. This sign indicates a document.

Easter: When Ure Vaeiko transmits the writing, his arm is represented in exactly the same way.

The wooden tablet, each carved side of which constitutes a document, is in the same language

But the following comparison is even more striking:

China: A peg used for making or writing.

Work done on the basis of indications received, in accordance with a copy; has the meaning of "model" or "to imitate."

Easter: Tomenika retranscribes the writing received from Ure Vaeiko: .

To show the similarity more clearly, I will reproduce these two pairs of signs, one above the other:

China:

Easter: [rongo-rongo glyph], which becomes [glyph] if we eliminate the double contours of Easter Island writing. That is why, of all the individuals we have encountered, Tomenika is the only one shown in this particular form: he is copying the *rongo-rongo* writing from a received model.

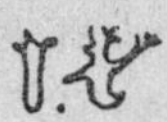

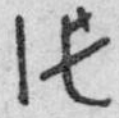

Finally, still within the framework of Chapter 9:

China: 世 Period of thirty years; represents the duration of a man's active life.

Easter: . [glyphs] . . Only now can we discern the deep meaning of these three ideograms, not separated by punctuation. As we have said, Ure Vaeiko received the writing from an initiate; he took a branch of the *toro miro* tree, squared it and made it into a tablet on which he carved the *rongo-rongo* signs. He then transmitted them.

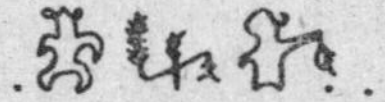

We can now say:

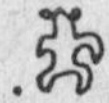

. [glyph] Ure Vaeiko

[glyph] spent his whole active life in studying *rongo-rongo* writing,

[glyph] and only at the end of that time did he also become an initiate (he is therefore represented in the guise of the birdman). He was then able to transmit the writing.

This interpretation explains why the scribe did not separate the three signs with dots.

ory of little Prince Rokoroko Hetau will show
r way in which Chinese writing is some-
armony with Easter Island legend.

In Chapter 11, dealing with the creation of the world, the god Make-Make . . is surrounded by stars .

Prince Rokoroko Hetau has two circles on his head. His *mana*, like a taboo, is indicated by these two superimposed groups of circles .

Chinese writing designates the stars by this sign: , "the quintessence of sublimated matter, which has risen to the sky and been crystallized there."

The three upper elements are the original sign, an image of the stars.

Here is the legend of Prince Rokoroko Hetau as it was told to me by Tila Mazière. This authentic version is highly significant because, for the first time, it shows the interest the Easter Islanders took in astronomy, and the importance they attached to the influence of the heavenly bodies in governing the life of the world. It also contains an important revelation concerning the *mana* of Easter Island.

I will quote Tila Mazière:

"There is a first indication in Rokoroko Hetau's which means 'In the time of . . .' or 'In the time when name. Polynesian legends begin with '*He tau* . . .'

. . .' At his birth, Rokoroko Hetau was not the legitimate heir, but the youngest son. Power always went to the eldest son, to whom the king, in this case Nga Ara, bequeathed his *mana*. But something highly unusual happened: the *mana* was transferred to the youngest son. This meant that the father, King Nga Ara, seemed to be losing his *mana*. To remedy that abnormal situation, he decided to kill the little prince.

"That was the time when the *mana* of the island began weakening. It finally disappeared at the death of the last king, the child Gregorio, who died in the leprosy hospital on the island in the nineteenth century. *He tau*: 'In the time when . . .'

"In *rongo-rongo* writing, Rokoroko Hetau is shown by this sign: . He bears those two *stars* because the transfer of such powerful *mana* to him evokes *the time when* the earth was under the influence of Gemini, the Twins, with their two most visible stars: Castor. and Pollux. There is a reminder of the time when the earth was under the influence of Gemini, *the time when mana* was installed."

But besides its time meaning, *he tau* also has a place meaning. It means "anchor" and, by extension, "to become installed." We will have occasion to discuss this later.

All this is thus indicated by the circles on Rokoroko Hetau's head, by the mark of his taboo; in other words, by the same signs that designate the stars in Chinese writing.

China: 知 Knowledge, which makes one capable of speaking on a subject with the precision of an arng its target. Hence the association of a

and a man pierced by an arrow .

Easter: the birdman, possessing Knowledge. We have the impression that this Knowledge is linked to the transportation of the statues by these ropes , which have the same shape as the Chinese sign. In China, Knowledge consisted in forming a judgment, indicated by this mouth ; on Easter Island it consisted in knowing how to move the statues by these ropes . But let me stress that this is only one aspect of Knowledge, as we will see.

A similar sign appears several times on the wooden tablets. It is also present in the writing of Mohenjo-Daro:

It is the mark of Knowledge, no matter what other figures may be associated with it in a given sign.

In the line relating the legend of King Nga Ara (Chapter 12), we saw that Rokoroko Hetau's birth was accompanied by extraordinary phenomena, particularly storms, which were indicated by lightning . All this was a bad omen, as were the sea animals that devoured people on the shore, and the appearance of white hens.

In China, fire, particularly in the form of lightning,

was regarded as a calamity. Lightning was written . The idea of "unfortunate" was expressed as (a man falling into a pit ,
with the meaning of misfortune).

The Easter Island sign can therefore be regarded as a combination of the two Chinese signs above — , in both form and meaning.

Easter (Chapter 13): Cord used for invoking ancestors; each knot corresponds to an ancestor.

China: The figure 2, figure of the earth, which forms a pair with the sky.

As can be seen on ancient bronze vases, the presence of an ancestor was often indicated by eyes: .

Let us associate the earth, two parallel lines ,
with the eyes indicating an ancestor .

Easter: This sign has been called, on Easter Island, "the eyes of the earth"; two parallel lines for the earth, circles for the eyes of the ancestor. An amazing similarity to the Chinese mode of expression, and a beautiful name for ancestors: "the eyes of the earth."

But, above all, we here see the deep meaning of the genealogical knotted cords (Chapter 13).

I will end this book with a return to the must now go beyond the first meaning of Island sign. For example, we have spoken of the convex base of the statue and its incantatory attitude, with arms raised toward the realm of the dead. Let us forget that immediate interpretation and try to find the second meaning by examining similarities between Chinese and Easter Island characters.

China: Ancient: that which has passed through ten mouths ; that is, through a tradition going back ten generations.

Easter: Statue seen from the front. The sign can be imagined without its double contours: . These statues were consecrated to worship of the ancestors, the Ancient Ones.

But this comparison is given only as an example; I will examine the following one in greater detail.

China: To try to know the future. It was believed that the future could be predicted by examining the cracks (the two perpendicular fissures) in a tortoise shell. is the sign for divination, the ability to foresee the future.

Easter: . [glyphs]. The Orongo statue (Chapter 4), seen in profile, facing the sea.

The Easter Islanders called it the "Statue With the Power to Balance Things," and not the "Wave Breaker," as has been claimed. They attributed to it the power of divination, the power to foresee the future and ward off calamities, to "harmonize events."

In China the symbol for water [glyph] was used to designate calamity, since an overflowing river was a calamity for the people who lived on its banks.

If the two preceding Chinese signs are placed side by side, we have an association between the ideas of divination and calamity:

Divinity [glyph] Calamity [glyph]

In Easter Island writing, the statue that had the power to foresee the future and ward off calamities is represented: . [glyphs].

In China, water [glyph] had the meaning of "calamity" only during a limited period. "When Tong Tso Pin established the succession of forms taken by the character for 'calamity,'" writes B. Tchang Tcheng Ming, "he showed that during the first three of the five periods of the Yin Dynasty, from Wu-ting (1323?–1269? B.C.) to Kang-ting (1240?–1219? B.C.), the character for 'calamity' was simply written as 'water' [glyph]."

In the case of the Orongo statue, the Easter Island sign . may have this second meaning; are we to conclude that the Asian influence in Hiva was manifested only during that same period, since the character for "calamity" in China later changed and associated fire with water?

The Chinese influence may have left its mark even after that time, however, since we have seen that the lightning announcing Rokoroko Hetau's birth also had the meaning of "unfortunate," as in Chinese writing , and therefore of "calamity," which later associated water with fire (and particularly lightning).

As we can see, it is very hard to date Hotu Matua's departure from Hiva. I had that in mind when I examined the two writings; it is a logical argument, since it was Hotu Matua who brought *rongo-rongo* signs to Easter Island. Other research will be necessary to establish that important point.

We will see, however, that a dominant element in this matter is based on one of the oldest Chinese signs. It is what makes me think that the twelfth-century date assigned to Hotu Matua's voyage is too late, although I cannot state it with certainty. Insofar as it is closely linked to the second-period statues, which were made after Hotu Matua's voyage, the problem of the first-period statues may become more complicated, unless they were intended to bear other attributes besides the signs on their backs; but we will discuss that later.

In any case, the time of the Chinese influence in Hiva is as important as the time of Hotu Matua's arrival on Easter Island.

It may be very ancient, and the character for "calamity" . [rongo-rongo character] . , used in isolation in *rongo-rongo* writing, may even place it in the fourteenth century B.C.

The position of the signs on the backs of the first-period statues, and of their hands, joined under the navel, may be explained by Chinese thought.

First, the position of the hands is of fundamental significance. Those statues immortalize life, in the stone of which they are made, by the current of energy that runs through them, as Tomenika showed us; the position of the hands indicates the point on the abdomen, the *she men*, where Chinese medicine situates the *ancestral* center of procreational energy and vitality. *She men*, or "stone door." In a Taoist concept, that point is the seat of immortality. That same immortality which was the goal of the Easter Island statues?

The statues bear a circle at the level of the sacrum. The word "sacrum" comes from the Latin *os sacrum*, "sacred bone." The ancient Romans gave it that name because it was the part of a sacrificial victim that was offered to the gods. But on Easter Island the meaning is different. Tila Mazière said to me, "*Hetau te mana*" ("*Mana* entered there").

Ancient Chinese medicine calls that part of the body *ming men*, "door of life."

Tila Mazière also told me that the little wooden statues bear two circles. One of them is at the level of the sacrum, but in this case the circle is closed by a dot. Being initially closed, it has the meaning of, "It is up to you to open it."

The second circle, without a dot, is at the level of the cervical vertebrae, "through which *mana* is expressed." Between the seventh cervical vertebra and the first thoracic vertebra is a very important point in Chinese medicine: the reunion point of all the yang meridians.

On some statuettes, however, the circle is on the head, in accordance with traditions that may be more recent, in which the head is the seat of *mana*.

The circle through which *mana* entered the stone statues is on their backs. Is this also one of the reasons why the second-period statues stand with their backs to Hiva, from which *mana* came? That idea does not contradict what was said about the orientation of the statues in Chapter 10. It simply approaches the problem on another level. It enables us to grasp the thought behind these signs in Chapter 6: . The statue stands with its back to the sea , which is the source of the *mana* that it will receive .

Can that source be a gigantic stone from which Knowledge emanated, since the "head" of the character is in three parts? Veriveri spoke of an enormous red volcanic stone which kept the power of the statues turned toward the south.

At this point it is important to make other distinctions between the two different types of statues.

The first-period statues at the foot of Rano Raraku are the ones that have hands with tapering fingernails and clear inscriptions on their backs. It was with regard to them that I spoke of an influence from Hiva, in discussing an Asian period added to the inspiration of the sculptors from the east. The term "Asian" refers only to the two features of the statues mentioned above; but their origin is in Hiva.

It was from there that Hotu Matua later came. Work in the quarry on the volcano was resumed, with a new tendency in the art and purpose of the statues. They were taken to the shore; hats of red volcanic stone were placed on their heads; eyes were made for them. Although their general appearance remained the same, however, degeneration had set in: their features are less harsh, more softened; their arms and hands are atrophied and no longer have the slender delicacy of the first statues. As for the signs on their backs, they are sometimes completely absent.

Within the framework presented in this book, that development is paradoxical. Since Hotu Matua's people had come from Hiva, it would be natural to think that they originated those specifically western (in relation to Easter Island) features of the statues: tapering fingernails and dorsal signs. But they found them already there when they arrived on the island.

But perhaps Hotu Matua came before the twelfth century, as I have suggested. That would not solve the problem, however, because it would not explain the change in the style of the second-period statues.

Or could the dorsal inscriptions have been part of a universal language in ancient times? But that would not explain the hands with long fingernails.

Must we assume a gap between the two periods? Was there not continuity, and evolution conditioned by other factors? Such as the parallel development of *rongo-rongo* writing, which was first inscribed on stone, and then on wood. Such as the appearance of the *moai kava-kava* statuary. But is this not the mark of a development that took place in Hiva in the meantime? It was later brought to Easter Island, where it may have given rise to changes closely related to the disappearance of the original homeland. There was a need to evoke the ancestors, with hats of red volcanic stone on the statues. And, to remain in contact with the vanished homeland, the statues had to have their backs to the sea, for it was through their backs that they received the *mana* which originated in Hiva.

We again encounter this major problem: between the Asian period (occurring between the earliest period and the first period) and the second period inaugurated by Hotu Matua, there was a change concerning Hiva, and the altered style of the statues is a direct reflection of it. *That change can only have been the disappearance of Hiva,* toward which the Easter Islanders then directed their whole work.

In a first phase, the statues at the foot of the volcano looked directly at Hiva, which then existed and was in the westerly direction of their gaze. In a second phase, the statues on the shore stood with their backs to Hiva, and in so doing they sought to go on receiving the *mana* that came "from beyond the sea" and penetrated them through the circles they bore on the lower part of their backs. *Hetau te mana.*

Comparison between ancient Chinese writing and Easter Island writing prompts me to return to two essential ideas: that of a transfer from China to Easter Island by way of Hiva, and that of a "common center" in Asia.

With regard to a Chinese influence in Hiva, all China specialists will be unanimous in saying that there was no possibility of any kind of direct transfer from ancient China to a Polynesian archipelago, especially one whose existence is only legendary. They will not have to look far for their major argument: Chinese seagoing junks did not appear until about the tenth century A.D.

I agree with that opinion. The transfer, as it can be deduced from comparison of the two writings, can only have been direct. The arrow on the map on page 177 is dictated by specific reasons, but its movement in a straight line from China to Hiva is an abstract notion.

I propose to reconsider that problem. But first I must date the Chinese characters I have mentioned. My reference author was Leon Wieger; the characters and their meanings are taken from his dictionary. As I have already said, it was not until I had "translated" thirteen lines of the Tomenika manuscript that I began looking for correlations with ancient Chinese writing, and when I had found similarities in shape between examples taken from both writings, what mattered most to me was the possibility of deriving the second meaning of each Easter Island sign from the first meaning of its corresponding Chinese sign.

It must be pointed out, however, that there is a time gap between the first appearance of the Chinese signs and such things as their meanings according to Wieger, the symbolism of long ears and hands with tapering fingernails, references to a Taoist concept, and so on. That gap seems to cover at least three centuries. All the elements mentioned are later than the fifth century B.C., and in my opinion that is too recent for a past that may have influenced Easter Island, because the Chinese characters appeared before the eighth century B.C.

I mentioned Wieger's interpretations because they were capable of shedding new light on the second meanings of the Easter Island characters; since there were similarities in shape between the two writings, I could not ignore elements that were likely to bring better understanding.

For example, some authors say that the Chinese character 世, with three foliages, has the meaning of "a generation," but Wieger says that its meaning is "the duration of a man's active life." That opened the possibility of interpreting the Easter Island sign , which also depicts three foliages, as "the duration of Ure Vaeiko's active life" (Chapter 15).

But Wieger may have drawn his interpretation of archaic Chinese writing from the works of Chinese scholars of the Han period, at the beginning of the Christian era, when Confucian influence was strong. I have cited these references; however, on the same basis as the symbolism of long ears or long fingernails (which imply meditation, since they show a lack of dependence on manual work), and on the same basis as the important acupuncture centers which are so disturbing when they are compared with the locations of the highly significant marks on Easter Island statues, because *it is permissible to believe that a symbolism or a system of thought may have appeared in oral tradition, whether mythical or grounded in concrete fact, long before its appearance in a form of writing, an applied doctrine or a work of art.*

I will now let myself be guided by the Easter Island signs. They have led to a relationship with forty Chinese signs which it is important to date. My reference here will be another work: *Grammata Serica*, by Bernhard Karlgren (Museum of Far Eastern Antiquities, Stockholm, Bulletin No. 12). The representations of archaic signs given by Karlgren are, on the whole, comparable to Wieger's, but he limits himself to more concise interpretations, closer to the initial meanings.

A comparative study of those two dictionaries would be beyond the scope of this book, but I will mention one example in passing. Cinnabar, red mercuric sulfide, a symbol of the alchemy that appeared in China after the fifth century B.C., was indicated by a dot in a melting pot, as we have seen. Karlgren shows that the bright red color known as vermilion was indicated in the same way, and that this sign dates from the Chou I period (1122–950 B.C.); and so, aside from alchemy, we come back to what has already been stated: the hat of red volcanic stone on the statues was indicated by a dot in Easter Island writing.

On the basis of Karlgren's work I will date the appearances of the Chinese characters mentioned in Chapters 8 and 15:

—Half of them are from the Shang period, before the twelfth century B.C.

—A quarter of them are from the Chou I period, 1122–950 B.C.

—An eighth of them are from the Chou II period, 950–770 B.C.

—Only one of them is from the Chou III period:  , an ovary, in the sense of an egg, which appears in the *Tso Shuan* (sixth to fifth centuries B.C.). I compared it with the Easter Island sign  , oviduct and egg. The analogy is striking, but it is hard to formulate a hypothesis on the basis of one sign. The correlation might be explained by the fact that the distinctive features of an object sometimes cause it to be given similar pictorial representations in different places; I have already spoken of such images of concrete realities.

—Only one of them is from the Chou IV period (450–250 B.C.):  plants, particularly herbaceous plants. I have compared it with the Easter Island sign for plants  , less because of a resemblance in shape than because of a common principle: the principle of indicating multiplicity by repetition of a phoneme, then drawing a sign that combines two identical elements. In China it goes back to very remote times.

In Easter Island writing there is often repetition of two identical elements to show the multiplicity of the objects involved. The father heating stones to be applied to the mother's belly after childbirth: he holds two of them in his hand (Chapter 3). Several sculptors for each statue: the writing shows two sculptors. And so on.

After these considerations, and especially the fundamental fact that most of the Chinese characters which show similarities to Easter Island characters appeared before the eighth century B.C., I will return to the question of a transfer from ancient China to Hiva. It must have begun earlier than the eighth century B.C. But what route did it follow?

I believe it took place by way of Southeast Asia. This hypothesis is based on two arguments:

a) In the Shang Period (seventeenth to twelfth centuries B.C.), marked by the appearance of bronze, the metals composing that alloy, particularly tin, reached northern China partly from the south. Cowries (small seashells that were used as money) also came from the south. So did the shells of giant tortoises; when they had been held over fire, the cracks in them were used in divination. J. Garnet points out that certain Shang bronzes, bearing representations of faces with Melanesian or Negroid features, also attest to the existence of relations between China and the countries of Southeast Asia in the Shang period.

Since there were trade routes from Southeast Asia to northern China, may we not assume that a certain number of graphic signs may have been brought into the south?

b) Southeast Asia was the starting point of the waves of migration that spread across the Pacific to Polynesia before the eighth century B.C.

May we not assume that one of those eastward migrations brought ancient Chinese signs to Hiva, from where they were later taken to Easter Island, first during what I have called the "Asian" period, then by Hotu Matua?

This question now arises: Why is it that on Easter Island, during that "Asian" period, symbols such as long ears and tapering fingernails were developed from the start, whereas in Asia, from which I believe they came, they did not appear until later? Perhaps because on Easter Island the great statues of the first period were the single, dominant preoccupation of the people, and were the medium best suited to the representation of such symbols.

Finally, I have spoken of a "common center in Asia" from which numerous civilizations were derived, particularly that of Easter Island. Since I have referred to such diverse origins and routes—from India to Hiva by way of Melanesia, from China to Hiva by way of Southeast Asia—that idea of a "common center" seems difficult to pin down. It appears more as an abstract entity than as a place of origin. But does it not take on reality at the end of the great journey, at the destination assigned to it by history on that "dot in the melting pot of the ocean" where the sublime fusion took place: Easter Island?

I tried to find in *rongo-rongo* writing a sign resem-

bling one of the oldest and most disturbing Chinese characters: this square with recessed corners: ⌗
It indicated the niche at the back of a temple from which the presence of ancestors emanated.* Its connection with ancestors was so basic that it was engraved on ancient Chinese vases.

I found it nowhere in Easter Island writing.

I thought back on what Francis Mazière was told on Easter Island about the group of seven statues that may have been erected to the memory of the seven explorers who preceded Hotu Matua's arrival: "Those statues are solemn twice a year, at the solstices." I concluded that there must be a connection between that sign ⌗ and the position of the sun, as though it could appear only under certain conditions of light.

That sign was present all over Easter Island, so much so that it conditioned the whole statuary of the second period.

At certain times of day the sun draws it perfectly: the shadows of the statues' hats come down to their deep, dark eye sockets and the sign stands out clearly against the sky,

*In Karlgren's view, the sign was linked to a family name, but that involves a reference to ancestors.

because those hats or red volcanic stone have that distinctive shape on top. It was from them that the presence of the ancestors emanated. In the time when man lived close to the forces of nature, that presence united him with the universe. And the people of Easter Island felt that deep union with the elements of the world.

It is that union which, all through this book, I have called Knowledge.

Easter Island, do you have more to tell us through your writing? More about the deep, hidden meaning of some of your signs?

The path of the statues was written ⊔ (Chapter 6). The ideogram is not closed. That path went toward eternity.

A life was written || . "One of the lines is birth, the other is death. Between the two is life." But how can we fail to notice that the sign is open at each end? The secret meaning that dwelt in those people is now revealed:

|| Birth was not a beginning. Death was not an end.

And life? Simply a path between two eternities.

EPILOGUE

So ends this inner voyage.

Nga Ara, Ure Vaeiko, Tomenika, Veriveri, your world and your writing were magnificent. Our writing has passed into abstraction. Yours has remained in beauty. That same beauty by which Chinese writing indicated the direction of your origin in Hiva, the west 西 : a bird in its nest, for in the evening, when the sun sets in the west, the bird rests in its nest.

This voyage to a unique place where everything is multiple.
A closed universe, yet one that opens into immensity.
In the depths of the dense, starry nights of Easter Island.
Above the flames that roar beneath volcanoes now extinct.

Across the greatest ocean, where Matakiterani glitters.
Like a precious stone, with all its radiance, fringed by the breaking surf.
With "the clouds, the marvelous clouds that pass, far away . . ."

The people looked at the sky, and rose to greatness.
The immense statues stood erect.

Then the people fell into unreason.
The statues were overthrown.

The inspiration for them came from South America.
The people were taken to mines off the coast of Peru.

To receive Knowledge, they became inhabited by the god, and embodied themselves in the birdman.
Only the bird could return to Hiva.

They approached Make-Make, the god of birds . . .
They died in guano mines.

But Matakiterani is not dead.
She awaits her new inhabitants.
Those whose hearts she invades.

Camerons to possess the black hair and eyes — a legacy from the dark gods, or so the stories go."

"The dark gods?"

"Druids," Maura smiled. "They either charm you or curse your life at birth, watch over you with a keen eye or laugh cruelly at each mistaken step. They certainly watched over Ewen. He was brash and arrogant, brave to the point of lunacy. He was the only Highland laird who dared refuse to submit to Cromwell's rule after King Charles was defeated back in 1649. He refused to take an oath of allegiance to a 'white-collared, cattle-lifting prelate' and even sent a demand to the new Parliament for remunerations, accusing the so-called New Model Army of destroying some of his fields and carrying away valuable livestock without paying for it."

"What did Cromwell do?" Catherine asked, well aware of the English reformer's swift and harsh justice for all rebels.

"He paid it. He also issued strict orders to his generals to stay clear of Cameron land."

Catherine raised her eyebrows delicately and studied the darkly handsome face again.

"They were inseparable, Ewen and Alex," Maura added. "I am surprised you have not heard all about him."

"To be honest — " Catherine set her jaw and turned to face Lady Cameron, the need to terminate the entire farce once and for all burning at the back of her throat. "To be honest — " The soft brown eyes were waiting expectantly, and Catherine's resolve faltered. "We have not known each other very long; he has not told me very much about anything. I had no idea what to expect when we arrived and, well, frankly, I had imagined all manner of — "

"Naked, bearded mountainmen?" Maura's laugh was directed more at herself than at Catherine. "I spent eight years in London, attending school. I know all too well the image most Englishmen have of Scotland and her people, and in some instances, it is well deserved. We are a proud and touchy breed, especially here in the Highlands where a man will draw his sword rather than shrug aside an insult. There are blood feuds that have carried on for centuries, some so long no one remembers the original cause."

"Like the Campbells and the Camerons?"

Maura drew back and for a moment looked as if she might drop the candle. But it only wavered in her hand, dripping hot wax over her fingers, which she did not seem to notice.

"I'm sorry," Catherine said quickly. "Did I say something wrong? I only asked because it was Campbell men who attacked us on the road today and a Campbell who seems bent on seeing Alexander hanged for murder."

This time Maura blanched. Her eyes flicked past Catherine's shoulder to the other two ladies, and she indicated by a shake of her head that they were not to say anything.

"Lady Cameron, I — "

"No, no you have not said anything wrong, dear. I was just not prepared . . . but of course, if Alexander has told you nothing about the family, you could not possibly be expected to know . . . to know that I am a Campbell."

"You?" As an image of the coarse, foul-breathed sergeant they had encountered earlier in the day flashed into Catherine's mind, she found it hard to make an association between him and the delicate, genteel Lady Cameron. Nor, from what she had begun to comprehend of clan warfare and blood feuds, should any member of an opposing clan have been allowed to set foot on the other's land and survive, let alone marry — and marry the clan chief! It was also disconcerting to realize one of Maura's relatives had fixed the price on Alexander Cameron's head, or had been directly responsible for the treachery of Gordon Ross Campbell.

There was simply too much going on that Catherine did not understand, too many complexities she did not *want* to understand. Her sense of isolation, her exhaustion came reeling down upon her with a vengeance and she raised a trembling hand to her forehead.

"Ye think tha's a shock, hen?" Auntie Rose muttered.